HOW TO MAKE CITIZEN INVOLVEMENT WORK

Strategies for Developing Clout

by Duane Dale
Citizen Involvement Training Project

The Citizen Involvement Training Project (CITP) is a project of the Cooperative Extension Service at the University of Massachusetts at Amherst. CITP is funded by a major grant from the W.K. Kellogg Foundation of Battle Creek, Michigan.

The contents of this manual are the sole responsibility of the author; endorsement of the content by the University of Massachusetts or sponsoring organizations should not be inferred.

© University of Massachusetts (Citizen Involvement Training Project) 1978

Permission to reproduce portions of this manual for non-commercial purposes will be granted on request. Credit should be given to the Citizen Involvement Training Project.

Thanks...

... to the other Citizen Involvement Training Project team members who have helped with this manual. All have contributed ideas and inspiration in one way or another. Those who have been most directly involved are Nancy Mitiguy, John Gondek, Rich Barnhart, Robbie Gordon, Dean Hudson and Sally Habana-Hafner.

Thanks to Heidi for tolerating a typewriter on our vacation, and for suggestions and support.

And a very special word of thanks to the people who read and commeted on this manual in manuscript:

- Henry Allen, Boston Community School, Boston, Massachusetts
- Nancy Brown, Citizen Resource Center, West Boylston, Massachusetts
- Ann Burgunder, Fordham-Tremont Community Mental Health Center, Bronx, New York
- Susan Carpenter, Rocky Mountain Center for the Environment, Denver, Colorado
- Britt Ellis, Ombuds Committe for Mental Retardation, Northampton, Massachusetts
- Jim Stanton, Institute for Responsive Education, Boston, Massachusetts

Their comments and suggestions have been very helpful in refining this manual; remaining shortcomings are of course the responsibility of the author.

Other CITP Training Manuals

There are seven other manuals in the CITP series. Single copies are $6.00 plus .50 postage, prepaid. Write for information about quantity discounts: CITP, 138 Hasbrouck, University of Massachusetts, Amherst MA 01003 (413) 545-2038

* **Power: A Repossession Manual; Issues and Strategies for Community Organizing,** by Greg Speeter
* **Planning, for a Change: A Citizen's Guide to Creative Planning and Program Development,** by Duane Dale and Nancy Mitiguy
* **The Rich Get Richer and the Poor Write Proposals,** by Nancy Mitiguy
  Working Together: A Manual for Helping Groups to Work More Effectively, by Bob Biagi
  We Interrupt This Program...A Citizen's Guide to Using the Media for Social Change, by Robbie Gordon
  Playing Their Game Our Way: How to Hold the Political Process Accountable to Citizen Needs, by Greg Speeter
  Beyond Experts: A Guide for Citizen Group Training, by Duane Dale with Dave Magnani and Robin Miller

* See page 91 for more information about the first three manuals.

JK 1764 .D34

ISBN 0-934210-04-7
Library of Congress Catalog Card Number: 79-624734

Production of this manual was definitely a team effort. Here's the proof:

Manual Design/Layout

Robbie Gordon
Sally Habana-Hafner
Nancy Mitiguy

Graphics

Community Press Features (cpf)
Dover Pictorial Archive Series
Other sources as noted

Graphics Research

Greg Speeter

Stats

Bob Biagi

Editing

Doug Anderson
Nancy Lerner
Ken Walker

Typesetting

Campus Center Print Shop,
University of Massachusetts

Proofreading

Brenda Yellock
Stan Rosenberg
Sally Habana-Hafner
Duane Dale

Paste-Up

Nancy Mitiguy
Sally Habana-Hafner
Duane Dale

Printing

Hamilton Newell, Inc.
Amherst, Mass.

CITP Staff

Eduardo Aponte
Bob Biagi
Duane Dale
Robbie Gordon
Sally Habana-Hafner
Diana Krauth
Dave Magnani
Nancy Mitiguy
Stan Rosenberg
Greg Speeter
Al Goldin
John Gondek
Dean Hudson
Robin Miller
Brenda Yellock
Anita Jeffery-Viera
Richard Barnhart
Koletta Kaspar
Jay Walsh

Highlights

Analyzing Citizen Involvement—some classic examples of effective and influential writing, including a condensed version of Sherry Arnstein's "Eight Rungs on the Ladder of Citizen Participation."

The Forms of Citizen Participation—description and evaluation of 68 different mechanisms of citizen participation, including government- and citizen-initiated forms. Special sections on participation in long-range planning and corporate decision-making.

Diagnosing Your Group's Citizen Involvement—a guided analysis of 10 key components of citizen group effectiveness, including membership, access to decision-makers, development of an independent "analysis" of problems, etc.

80 Ways to Enhance Your Group's Clout—a "laundry list" of possible strategies to make a group more effective.

Contents

Thanks i
The Citizen Involvement Training Project iii
About the CITP Manual Series iii
About the Exercises iii

Part I: Public Policy — Who Decides?

The Citizen's Role in Policy Decisions 1
Advocates for Participation: An American Tradition 3
A Thumbnail History of Citizen Involvement: Two Views 4
A Personal History of Citizen Involvement (exercise) 6
Optimist or Pessimist? 7
Looking for Patterns in Citizen Action (exercise) 8
Analyzing Citizen Involvement: Some Classic Examples ... 9
"Eight Rungs on the Ladder of Citizen Participation," by
   Sherry R. Arnstein 10
The Concept of Cooptation: Philip Selznick, Roland Warren
   and Lord North 14
"Is This Any Way to Start a Revolution?" by Edward Schwartz. 15
"The Power Broker," by Robert Caro 17
The Accountability Problem 18
"The Crisis of Democracy," by Samuel P. Huntington 18
Issues in Citizen Involvement 20
Participation Dilemmas 20
Taking Stands on Participation Dilemmas (exercise) 21
What's Not Getting Dealt With 22
The Crucial Issues of Our Times 24
Options and Obstacles 26
The Forms of Citizen Participation 26
Visions for Citizen Involvement 44
Diagnosing Your Group's Involvement in Decision-Making ... 48

Part II: Taking Action for Better Citizen Involvement

Introduction 56
New Structures 57
A Watchdog Group for Citizen Participation 57
Setting Up a New Citizen Participation Organization 59
Improving on the Organization You've Got 67
The Transition to Citizen Power (exercise) 68
Developing Transition Strategies 70
Holding an Agency to Its Citizen Participation Guidelines
   (exercise) 71
Developing Real Input into Policy (a workshop plan) 72
80 Ways to Enhance Your Group's Clout 77
Notes to the Individual Citizen 81
Choosing Your Issue 82
Questions to Ask 83
Voting with Your Feet: When and How to Quit 85
Sticking with It 85

Resources 86

ii

The Citizen Involvement Training Project

The Citizen Involvement Training Project is a three-year project of the Cooperative Extension Service, University of Massachusetts at Amherst. Funded by the W.K. Kellogg Foundation, CITP provides training workshops, materials, and consultations to citizen groups throughout Massachusetts. The staff of nine includes specialists in organizing, fund-raising, group process, planning methods, information gathering, social change, and adult education, and offers bilingual training as well.

CITP services include workshops and consultation, a 1000-volume Citizen Involvement Library (available to individuals and citizen groups), staff-generated manuals (such as this) and a "Training of Trainers" workshop series intended to help citizen groups establish their own training components in their communities.

CITIZEN INVOLVEMENT
TRAINING PROJECT
138 Hasbrouck
Cooperative Extension Service
University of Massachusetts
Amherst, Massachusetts 01003
(413) 545-2038

About the CITP Manual Series

Because the participants are the most essential resource for citizen training, it is sensible to consider the possibility of citizen training without the presence of "professional" trainers. And because there are people in nearly every citizen group who are aware of the need for skill-building and consciousness-raising, people with the insight and leadership skills to promote citizen training programs, it seems perfectly feasible to promote a self-sufficient approach to training.

This manual, as well as others in the series, is intended to help citizen groups set up their own on-the-job training activities tailored to their individual needs, issues, learning styles and experiences. It is also hoped that these manuals will be used to help orient new members to an organization and will be an integral part of membership/staff development. In writing these guides we have used what we have learned through our experience with hundreds of citizen groups to help you ask yourselves questions which will tap both universal and unique citizen group problems.

Those citizen group members who have participated in a CITP workshop (or some other training workshop) will be able to use the manuals as a back-home resource to continue personal skill-building or to share it with others. Activities and information described in the manuals, however, have also been geared to those who have never had personal contact with CITP or other training agencies.

Some organizations are reluctant to spend time on training activities, at least before the merits have been proven. The reluctance is appropriate; training can be a diversion from the real concerns of the group. But training activities can focus so directly on those "real concerns" that progress toward more long-range goals is made during the training; doing and learning can become almost indistinguishable.

If you are the one introducing training exercises to your group, first you might want to spend some time discussing these reluctances or individual learning preferences. Then again, you may want to let the proof of the pudding rest in the tasting.

About the Exercises

Several sections in this manual are labeled in the Contents as "exercises." This means that they are designed for use by a group of citizens as a way to develop skills, try out a structured planning process, etc. In addition, most sections have discussion questions which provide the basis for group use of this manual.

The ideal setting for most of these activities would be groups of five to eight people. Larger groups can be accommodated by dividing into smaller groups if necessary, and of course one person can use the discussion questions and most of the exercises. For groups, you may want to duplicate selected sections, re-sequencing them if you wish, and perhaps reassembling them into a condensed training workbook for your particular group.

Whatever way you use the manual, we hope you will tailor it to suit your own needs and learning styles. You and your group are in the best position to judge what will be useful and appropriate. You are the ones who can integrate the activities into the on-going problem-solving and skill building within your group. This manual is a tool to help you do that.

PART I: PUBLIC POLICY —WHO DECIDES?

The Citizen's Role in Policy Decisions

In every community, dozens of decisions are made daily which affect the lives of the local citizens and often the lives of people around the globe: whether to add a new wing to the hospital; whether to cut the school budget; whether to install pollution control devices in a factory's smokestacks; whether to move a factory to a developing country where labor is cheaper. And of course there are decisions being made in various centers of power which also affect every community — decisions made on Capitol Hill, Madison Avenue, Wall Street, Detroit, the Pentagon, the White House and elsewhere. The decision makers are primarily politicians and corporate executives; they are influenced more often than not by influential people like themselves.

The widespread concern for developing more and better mechanisms for citizen involvement is really a concern that the voice of the ordinary citizen be heard in these public policy questions. The recent proliferation of citizen boards, councils, issue-organizations, movement groups, etc. indicate concern that the voice of the public (or some part of the public) be heard in public policy decisions.

But numbers of citizen groups or citizen activists do not guarantee success. Many citizen groups are "advisory," with no significant influence. Many others have no access to decision makers at all.

A very important part of making citizen involvement work is for citizens in every community to monitor, analyze and criticize the quality of citizen involvement activities in their communities. These people would be citizen advocates—watchdogs of the advisory boards, the environmental groups, the conservation commissions, the taxpayer councils — observing their success in accurately and influentially representing the public's views so as to change the shape of public policy decisions. And because the success of citizen involvement is indicated by its effect on decisions, our citizen involvement analysts will also need to scrutinize public policy decision-making, wherever it takes place, to ask again and again the basic question, "Who decides?" Does a decision reflect the public's best interests or those of a small and privileged group?

Imagine that every community has even a half-dozen people who conscientiously monitor the public policy decisions in their community, people who persistently ask, "Who decides?" Even this handful of critics can keep decision-makers on their toes and help their fellow citizen activists find ways to be more effective.

If these citizen critics or monitors were articulate

about their concerns, the mass media would begin to pursue them. Already, there are Moscow-watchers and Cuba-watchers, election analysts and sports specialists. So we might envision a time when every newspaper has its citizen involvement column, and every radio station has its regular talk show guest . . .

Moderator: Welcome to **Open Mouth**. Tonight's guest is Ms. Jane Pleasant, a self-styled "citizen advocate" who believes there should be community representatives on the Jamestown Shoe Corporation's Board of Directors. Tell us, Jane, how you came to that conclusion . . . .

New Unity

"For too long, I have been guilty of the crime of silence."

On the national level, Ralph Nader and John Gardner are the most visible of the people who take on the role of public policy watchdog and citizen advocate. At the state and local levels, there are people who monitor decision-making and advocate for the public, but there could be a lot more. Who would the citizen involvement advocate, the public decision monitor, be? Potentially, any of thousands of local citizen activists—people who already have an intimate, well-informed view of citizen participation and public policy. We hope that some of you who are reading this manual will choose that role.

What does it take to be an effective watchdog of public policy decisions and citizen involvement mechanisms?

- An interest in citizen involvement; a real commitment to the success of democratic self-government

- A historical perpective; a sense of the development of democratic forms and citizen participation mechanisms

- A sense of what's possible; visions for the future, and a feel for practical alternatives that could improve a specific effort or the overall citizen participation within a community

- A familiarity with the terms and issues raised in relation to citizen involvement

- A list of questions that you will want to raise regarding citizen participation—for one group or a community

- Practice in making judgments about citizen involvement

- A sense of what you can do with the information you gather and the judgments you make

The interest and commitment will have to come from you; if you've got them, this manual will help you with the rest. Part I is a tool kit—information, exercises, questionnaires, a glossary and other ideas to help you effectively analyze citizen paticipation and public policy in your organization and your community.

Your local paper won't necessarily begin quoting you as its favorite "well-informed source." (You may decide that's not the most useful thing to do with your analysis anyway.) But you will be better prepared to make judgements about how to make citizen involvement work and better prepared to go on to Part II which will deal with **action** citizens can take to improve the quality and effectiveness of citizen participation.

Advocates for Participation: An American Tradition

The idea of citizens monitoring the functioning of government and evaluating the quality of citizen participation has roots in the American Revolutionary period. The Declaration of Independence asserted for all citizens the right to determine whether a government is fulfilling its intended purposes and also, if a government becomes destructive of its intended ends,

"The right to alter or to abolish it, and to institute new government."

These strong words came not only from the fiercely democratic principles of Thomas Jefferson; they were the product of years of growing criticism of the British governance of the colonies.

"The sole end of government is protection and security of the people. Whenever, therefore, that power which was originally instituted to effect these important and valuable puposes is employed to harass, distress, or enslave the people, in this case it becomes a curse rather than a blessing."
-Provincial Congress of Massachusetts, 1774

Of course, not all the revolutionary leaders agreed on the forms or the level of power which citizens should have. The debates of the Constitutional Convention centered in part around this issue. There was also, for example, the continuing debate between Jefferson, the democrat, and Hamilton, the efficient administrator. Jefferson minced no words in explaining how he saw the two sides of the debate.

"Men by their constitutions are naturally divided into two parties: (1) Those who fear and distrust the people, and wish to draw all powers from them into the hands of the higher classes. (2) Those who identify themselves with the people, have confidence in them, cherish and consider them as the most honest and sane, although not the most wise depository of the public interests. In every country these two parties exist; and in every one where they are free to think, speak and write, they will declare themselves."
-Thomas Jefferson, Letter to Henry Lee; August 10, 1824

Some critics of citizen involvement, then as now, claimed that the masses were often not well enough informed to vote intelligently. Jefferson responded,

"I know of no safe depository of the ultimate powers of this society but the people themselves; and if we think them not enlightened enough to exercise their control with a wholesome discretion, the remedy is not to take it from them, but to inform their descretion."
-Thomas Jefferson, Letter to William Charles Jarvis; September 28, 1820

A Thumbnail History of Citizen Involvement: Two Views

Recent publications on citizen involvement imply that the current interest in citizen participation is an outgrowth of the social unrest of the 1960s. The reality, of course, is a long history of public involvement in society's political and economic governance, dating back to the beginning of civilization. Here are two versions of the history of citizen involvement, starting from different assumptions and emphasizing different events.

Version 1: The essence of citizen involvement is democratic self-governance. Therefore, the history of citizen involvement is the history of the evolution of democratic institutions. It's a history of slow but steady progress toward full equality and orderly democratic governance.

Key Events in the Development of Democratic Institutions

- Republic, Greece, 600 B.C. (Council of Elders - aristocrats)

- Constitutional Democracy (limited) in Athens, 510 B.C.

- Origin of Parliament, England, 991 A.D.

- Jury Trial, England, 1176

- Rule by Law - Magna Carta, England, 1215

- Origin of House of Commons, England, 1254

- Bill of Rights, England, 1689

- Public Meetings, England, 1769

- U.S. Bill of Rights, 1791

- Ombudsmen, Sweden, 1809

- Abolition of Slavery in England, 1833 (U.S., 1863)

- Suffrage for Blacks in U.S., 1870

- Secret Ballot, England, 1872

- First Nation to Provide Suffrage for Women, New Zealand, 1893 (U.S., 1919)

Version 2: The history of citizen involvement is the history of people's persistent efforts to be heard. Forms of government have changed through the ages, but the poor and the disadvantaged are always with us and the wealthy and advantaged always do their best to ignore them.

People's Movements and Tactics

- Use of the Strike, Roman Plebs, 490 B.C. (for safeguards for debtors, right to intermarry with Patricians, right to vote)

- Trade Union, New Castle, England, 1699

- Tax Revolt: Boston Tea Party, 1770

- American Revolution, 1776-1783

- Farmer's Revolt: Daniel Shays' Rebellion, 1786

- First Peace Movement in U.S., 1815

- Abolitionist Movement in the U.S., 1830-1863

- Women's Suffrage Movement: First Convention, Seneca Falls, New York, 1848

- Pullman Strike (first major industrial strike in the U.S.), 1899

- Sit-in for Civil Rights, Chicago, 1942

- Freedom Riders, 1961 (blacks and whites riding together on buses to test the right to unsegregated service in interstate transit)

- Civil Rights Marches and Demonstrations, Albany, Georgia, 1962

- Women's Liberation Movement: National Organization of Women founded, 1966

- Welfare Rights Organization, U.S., 1967

- Consumer Rights Movement, U.S., 1960s

- Modern Environmental Movement, U.S., ca. 1970

Version 1 is a history of developing institutions; Version 2 emphasizes the steps, the processes, which led to institutional changes. For example, equal voting rights for women became the law in New Zealand in 1893 and in the U.S. in 1919. Version 1 emphasizes the institutional change (the Nineteenth Amendment to the U.S. Constitution, for example), whereas Version 2 would, if space allowed, detail the conventions, the marches, the speeches, the lobbying and even the husband-and-wife debates which contributed to the change.

Version 1 is primarily a history of decision-makers—those who passed and ratified the Nineteenth Amendment, for example. The principle roles in Version 2 were played by ordinary citizens—some of whom rose to national stature, such as Elizabeth Cady Stanton and Susan B. Anthony, but most of whom remain anonymous. Version 1 might suggest that the politicians initiated the social changes; Version 2 documents the groundswell of public concern that led to the changes.

Version 1 might be seen as the continuing march of progress in the development of democratic forms. Version 2 shows the common people returning to old tactics or inventing new ones, participating in an on-going struggle to secure their rights. Some would see Version 2 as progress through on-going struggle; others would see it as an indication that things never really change.

Discussion Questions:

- *How do you view history—more like Version 1 or Version 2?*

- *What difference can the average citizen make in the course of events? What about many citizens acting together?*

- *Do you see continuing progress toward more democratic forms of governance and policy-making? Do you see progress only through on-going struggle? Or do you side with the French skeptic who said, "The more things change, the more they stay the same"?*

New Unity/cpf

Exercise:

A Personal History of Citizen Involvement

no. people: 5 to many
min. time: 30 minutes
materials: paper and pencil; copies of the previous section ("A Thumbnail History of Citizen Involvement: Two Views")

Writing a personal history of citizen involvement is a first step which can lead you to 1) some new insights about what worked and what was satisfying to you and 2) a sense of your part in the larger flow of events.

Process:

1. Each participant should read "A Thumbnail History of Citizen Involvement: Two Views."

2. Next, participants should spend five to ten minutes writing a thumbnail history of their own personal involvement in social concerns. Use the same format as the thumbnail histories, Versions 1 and 2; a sample is provided. If time allows, think about the discussion questions which follow.

3. In groups of five to eight, share your personal histories and then the answers to the discussion questions.

A Sample Personal History of Citizen Involvement

- *Worked for black City Council candidate in Chicago, 1967*

- *Worked with black neighborhood organization in Lexington, Kentucky; summer, 1967*

- *Helped found information/counseling center for people seeking meaningful work, 1970*

- *Helped write directory of Boston movement groups and alternative institutions, 1971*

Discussion Questions:

- *Which of your activities was most useful or productive?*

- *Least useful or productive?*

- *Why?*

- *In which activities were you most supported by others? Why and how?*

- *What do you do when your chosen methods do not seem to be achieving your goal?*

- *How long do you tend to work with one particular organization? With one issue?*

- *Is your personal history more similar to Version 1 or Version 2?*

- *Imagine that your current efforts succeed, and that they result in an event that should be listed in Thumbnail History Version 1 or Version 2. What would that listing say?*

Optimist or Pessimist?

The 1770s were clearly a time when many American colonials were becoming critical of the British control of the colonies. Other points in history can be identified during which most people were critical of government or of their lack of opportunity to be heard. But at any single point in time there are generally people who are optimistic or accepting and others who are pessimistic or critical.

Consider, for example, the two different interpretations which are currently given of the citizen involvement activities organized by the Army Corps of Engineers. The Corps gets involved in large-scale construction projects, especially in conjunction with the nation's waterways, such as dams, bridges and canals. Some people praise the Corps as a leader in citizen involvement—an agency that recognized decades ago that it needed Congressional support to continue its programs and that it needed the people's support in order to be persuasive with the legislators. So it developed a commitment to holding public meetings and heeding what the people said.

Others will tell you that the Corps is one of the worst agencies around. That environmentally, it is committed to damming every river in the country, no matter what that does to local ecosystems or flood plains. They contend that the Corps' citizen involvement program is mostly window dressing — a pretense of participation which provides the public only partial information about the problems of projects.

We suspect that many people take either the accepting or the critical view out of personal predisposition rather than thoughtful consideration of the facts. If you can't trust anyone from Washington or anyone who wears a uniform, you're a birthright critic, but if you're convinced that "our leaders are the finest men," you'll have a hard time answering questions posed by skeptics.

Test your predispositions; do you agree or disagree with the viewpoint expressed below? It is paraphrased from the words of one of CITP's clients, who shall remain anonymous.

The Certified Citizen

"The main purpose of citizen advisory boards is to give an agency the chance to choose who it wants to work with — to 'certify' the citizens who they think are smart enough, experienced enough, polite enough, cooperative enough. Whether it's the Mayor, or a state agency or a federal department which sets up citizen participation activity, they will pick the polite, cooperative citizens who are willing to consider things from the official perspectives. They may choose one token dissenter, but they'll leave out the real radicals, the less educated, the truly innovative, the brusque, the insistent citizens. They can say 'we are already taking the citizen's views into account' and brush off the ideas and criticisms of independent citizens. And even if the agency doesn't **appoint** the members of its citizen advisory board, it will attract the ones who are willing to 'play the game', the ones who are willing to attend meeting after meeting and review agency programs, policies and budgets.

"Things would really be better if there were no such thing as an official citizen advisory board. Then it wouldn't be so easy for an agency to listen only to its 'certified,' legitimated citizen representatives and ignore the rest. If we had no citizen boards at all, there would be more clamor of competing citizen voices, but the agencies wouldn't find it so easy just to listen to a few and ignore the rest."

Discussion Questions:

- *Do you know of agencies which seem to have this attitude toward citizen participation?*

- *Do you know of citizen boards which "channel" citizen input as described in the quotation, regardless of whether the agency planned it that way?*

- *Do you agree that things would be better off if there were no agency-created citizen boards?*

Exercise:

Looking for Patterns in Citizen Action

no. people: 1 to many
min. time: 30 minutes
materials: copies of the following scenarios

Citizen groups get bogged down in many ways. It's an important skill to be able to spot the dynamics and patterns by which citizen groups are denied power. The six discussion questions below constitute an analysis process which can be used by one person, but which is more effective in a group discussion format. After you have applied these questions to the scenarios here, you may want to identify and label patterns which your group has itself run up against.

The next section will have examples of the writings of established critics of citizen involvement processes; also, there is a glossary later in Part I. After you have read those sections, you may want to return to these scenarios and see whether you have acquired some new insights.

Process:

1. If a number of people are doing this excercise, they should form groups, preferably of five to eight people per group. Each group should identify someone to serve as facilitator for the discussion portion.

2. Each participant should read the vignette selected for study and answer the questions.

3. In a group discussion, compare answers to the questions and other reactions to the vignette.

Situation 1: The scene is a medium-large American city with a sizable population of Blacks, Puerto Ricans and other minority people, plus several neighborhoods of low income white families. Until recently, there had been no success at organizing these groups for anything more significant than recreation and block parties.

Recently, a bright and confident Puerto Rican woman began receiving support from the Spanish-speaking community for her complaints about the quality of public housing, and her proposal for cooperative ownership and management of the units by the neighborhood. Her name appeared in the paper for her statements at several public hearings.

Soon thereafter, ths woman was offered a paid position with the City's Housing Authority, which she accepted. Her friends and supporters chided her for selling out to the establishment and for abandoning her proposal for cooperative control of housing. Her consistent reply was that it's best to work as close as possible to where the decisions are made, and that it's worth some sacrifice to be able to do that.

Discussion Questions:

- *What's going on? What is the problem?*

- *Have you ever been in a situation like this? If so, describe what happened.*

- *How was your situation similar to or different from the vignette?*

- *How did you feel about the events you experienced?*

- *What was the outcome?*

- *What would you do about similar situations in the future?*

Situation 2: A group of citizens in the northeast corner of Dayville formed a Health Action Committee (HAC) two years ago. Since then they have started several health education programs, including workshops on nutrition, health for elders, maternity and overcoming addictions. They also studied occupational health problems of area residents. Their main project, however, is to create a local clinic for northeast Dayville because the city's two hospitals are a 20-minute drive or 40-minute bus ride away.

The committee proposed that the larger hospital move part of its outpatient facilities to a storefront in the community. A small family foundation had expressed interest in covering a major share of the remodeling costs, but the hospital's director and board kept coming up with reasons why the plan wouldn't work: complications with laboratory testing, duplication of records, questions about the need. In each case, a friendly M.D. helped HAC prepare a response. Just before the fourth round of negotiations, the hospital board announced plans for a $12 million expansion at its main site.

Discussion Questions:

- *What's going on? What is the problem?*

- *Have you ever been in a situation like this? If so, describe what happened.*

- *How was your situation similar to or different from the vignette?*

- *How did you feel about the events you experienced?*

- *What was the outcome?*

- *What would you do about similar situations in the future?*

Situation 3: Lake District Charities is a long-standing charitable foundation which administers some $2.7 million each year in grants to social and educational programs. According to one trustee, part of the foundation's job is to promote coordinated social service strategies throughout the region. "Also, we have to screen out approaches that obviously aren't going to work well. We often tell a group 'no' the first time they come to us, so that they'll be challenged to dig for grassroots support and also to demonstrate viability and commitment.

"As far as program design, we see it as our obligation to pass along the insights that we've acquired out of years of supervising projects. For example, para-professional social service programs are fine — up to a point. But it's absolutely essential for trained professional, such as psychiatrists or social workers, to direct and predominate in social service delivery.

"And then, last year, we had several applications in job training — which is definitely outside our area — and one group wanted to start a worker-owned manufacturing corporation, which would have put them in competition with local businessmen . . . and so an important part of our job is to advise groups as to what's appropriate, feasible and fundable."

Discussion Questions:

- *What's going on? What is the problem?*

- *Have you ever been in a situation like this? If so, describe what happened.*

- *How was your situation similar to or different from the vignette?*

- *How did you feel about the events you experienced?*

- *What was the outcome?*

- *What would you do about similar situations in the future?*

Analyzing Citizen Involvement: Some Classic Examples

Although the popular media haven't started quoting their local "citizen involvement watchers," more and more is being written about public participation. Government agencies have hired consultants to study possible responses to the demands for more citizen input; people with experience in government programs or citizen groups have felt inspired to write about their observations; academics interested in public policy have tackled the subject. In the next few pages we present some classic examples of good or otherwise noteworthy writings about citizen involvement. The major question, the overall question, is whether you might ever want to write in this style about citizen involvement as you see it. Would it be helpful to others in your community—decision-makers, activist citizens, and the uninvolved—to read and consider the experiences and observations of someone uninvolved in trying to influence public policy?

Eight Rungs on the Ladder of Citizen Participation

by Sherry R. Arnstein

Since it first appeared in 1969, Sherry Arnstein's article has been reprinted in many of the books on citizen participation, and with good reason. It deals with the basic consideration of how much power citizens have, by spelling out eight possible categories or levels of involvement. Ms. Arnstein was citizen participation advisor to the Model Cities Administration (Department of Housing and Urban Development) beginning in the late 1960s, and has consulted with most of the federal agencies which are dealing with new strategies for citizen participation.

What follows is a condensed version of the article, reprinted by permission of the Journal of the American Institute of Planners, *vol. 35, no. 4, July, 1969.*

The idea of citizen participation is a little like eating spinach: no one is against it in principle because it is good for you. Participation of the governed in their government is, in theory, the cornerstone of democracy—a revered idea that is vigorously applauded by virtually everyone. But when the have-nots define participation as redistrubution of power, the American consensus on the fundamental principle explodes into many shades of outright radical, ethnic, ideological, and political opposition.

Many authors and speech writers have explored in detail **who** are the have-nots of our time and **why** they have become offended and embittered by their powerlessness. However, scant attention has been paid to **what** citizen participation and is what its relationship is to the social imperatives of our times.

My answer to the critical **what** questions is simply that citizen participation is a categorical term for citizen power. The redistribution of power enables the have-not citizens—now excluded from the political and economic processes—to be deliberately included in the future. It is the means by which they determine how goals and policies are set, tax resources allocated, programs operated and contracts parceled out. It is the means by which significant social reform is induced.

Without the redistribution of power, however, participation is an empty and frustrating process for the powerless. It allows power holders to claim that all sides were considered when only a few will benefit. In an attempt to cut across the euphemisms and bombast of citizen participation, this typology presents eight different levels of participation in planning and operating public programs. The eight-rung ladder is a simplification that helps illustrate a vital point—that there are significant gradations of citizen participation. Thus the bottom rungs—manipulation and therapy—describe levels of "non-participation" that have been contrived by some to substitute for the genuine participation of many. In contrast, the top-most rungs—delegated power and citizen control—describe majority decision-making or full managerial power.

It should be noted that the typology does not analyze the most significant roadblocks to genuine levels of participation. On the powerholder's side, these roadblocks include racism, paternalism and resistance to power redistribution. On the have-not's side, they include the poor communities' inadequate political and economic infrastructure and knowledge base, plus their difficulties organizing a representative and accountable citizens group in the face of futility, alienation, and distrust.

1. **Manipulation**

In the name of citizen participation, people are placed on rubber-stamp advisory committees to "educate" them or engineer their support. Participation is distorted into a public relations vehicle by power-holders. An example of this manipulation has been community action agencies (CAAs) which create neighborhood councils with no legitimate function or power. These groups are used by the CAAs to "prove" that "grassroots people" are involved in the program. Most often, the program has not been discussed with the people or important information is left out. Only after the ribbon-cutting ceremony do the members of the council realize that they didn't ask the important questions, and that the bureaucratic web has only become stronger.

2. **Therapy**

This form of citizen participation is both dishonest and arrogant. Its administration assumes that powerlessness is synonymous with mental illness. Under the masquerade of involving citizens in planning, the experts subject the citizens to clinical group therapy. The focus is to cure them of their "pathology" rather than changing the racism and victimization that creates their "pathologies."

Common examples may be seen in public housing programs where tenant groups are used to promote control-your-child or clean up campaigns. The tenants are brought together to help them "adjust their values and attitudes to those of the larger society." Under these ground rules, they are diverted from dealing with such important matters as arbitrary evictions, segregation of the housing project, or why it takes three months to get a broken window replaced in winter.

3. **Informing**

Information about rights, responsibilities, and options is important for citizen participation; however, this frequently becomes a one way flow from official to citizen. No channel is provided for feedback and no power for negotiation. Excessively technical information, discouraging questions, and irrelevant answers are common tactics for turning meetings into vehicles for one way communication. Also, information may be presented at a late stage in planning, giving people little opportunity to influence the program design "for their benefit."

4. **Consultation**

If consulting is not combined with other modes of participation, it offers no assurance that citizen concerns and ideas will be taken into account. Attitude surveys, neighborhood meetings, and public hearings are frequently used to consult people.

If citizen input is restricted at this level, participation remains just a window-dressing ritual with people primarily perceived as statistical abstractions. Attitude surveys have become a particular bone of contention in ghetto neighborhoods. Residents are increasingly unhappy about the number of times per week they are surveyed about their problems and hopes. As one woman put it: "Nothing ever happens with those damned questions, except the surveyor gets $3 an hour, and my washing doesn't get done that day."

5. **Placation**

At this level citizens begin to have some degree of influence, though tokenism is still apparent. An example of placation strategy is to place a few hand picked "worthy" poor on boards of community action agencies or on public bodies like the Board of Education, Police Commission, or Housing Authority. If they are not accountable to the constituency in the community and if the traditional power elite hold the majority of seats, the have-nots can be easily outvoted and outfoxed. Other committees allow citizens to advise or plan, but retain for powerholders the right to judge the legitimacy or feasibility of the advice. The degree to which citizens are actually placated, of course, depends largely on the quality of technical help they have in articulating their priorities and on the extent to which the community has been organized to press for these priorities.

By and large, people are still being planned **for**. In most situations the major planning decisions are being made by agency staff and approved in a formalistic way by policy boards.

6. **Partnership**

At this rung of the ladder, power is redistributed

through negotiation between citizens and powerholders. They agree to share planning and decision-making responsibilities through such structures as joint policy boards, planning committees, and mechanisms for resolving impasses. After the ground rules have been established through some form of give-and-take, they are not subject to unilateral change.

Partnership can work most effectively when there is an organized power base in the community to which the citizen leaders are accountable and when the group has the financial resources to pay its leaders as well as hire technicians, lawyers, and community organizers. One community leader described it as "coming to City Hall with hat on head instead of in hand."

In most cases where power has come to be shared it was taken by the citizens, not given by the city. There is nothing new about that process. Since those who have power normally want to hang on to it, historically it has had to be wrested by the powerless rather than proffered by the powerful.

7. Delegated Power

Negotiations between citizens and public officials can also result in citizens achieving dominant decision-making authority over a particular plan or program. Policy boards on which citizens have a clear majority of seats and genuine specified powers are typical examples. At this level, citizens hold the significant cards to assure accountability of the program to them. To resolve differences, powerholders need to start the bargaining process rather than respond to pressure from the other end. Another model of delegated power is that of separate and parallel groups of citizens and powerholders, with provision for citizen veto if difference of opinion cannot be resolved through negotiation. This is a particularly interesting co-existence model for hostile citizen groups too embittered towards City Hall as a result of past "collaborative efforts" to engage in joint planning.

8. Citizen Control

Demands for community-controlled schools, black control, and neighborhood control are increasing. People are simply demanding that degree of power (or control) which guarantees that participants or residents can govern a program or an institution, be in full charge of policy and managerial aspects, and be able to negotiate the conditions under which "outsiders" may change them.

A neighborhood corporation with no intermediaries between it and the source of funds is the model most frequently advocated. A small number of such experimental corporations are already producing goods and/or social services. Several others are reportedly in the development stage, and new models for control will undoubtedly emerge as the have-nots press for more power over their lives.

8	Citizen Control	
7	Delegated Power	Degrees of Citizen Power
6	Partnership	
5	Placation	
4	Consultation	Degrees of Tokenism
3	Informing	
2	Therapy	
1	Manipulation	Nonparticipation

The Concept of Cooptation: Philip Selznick, Roland Warren and Lord North

When a large governmental agency becomes committed to a goal, it will often develop strategies for absorbing opposition. This was very much the case with the development of the Tennessee Valley Authority during the 1930s, with its widespread and interrelated projects for water power, flood control and community development. Local centers of opposition could be seen not only as threats to the agency-wide success but also as contrary to the growing community support throughout the region.

Philip Selznick's book, **TVA and the Grassroots,** studied the interaction between the agency and the local people. Selznick identified one of TVA's main ways of dealing with opposition as "cooptation" and in fact Selznick gave the phrase its technical meaning, which has now become fairly common in the popular language of citizen participation:

> "...[Cooptation is] the process of absorbing new elements into the leadership or policy-determining structure of an organization as a means of averting threats to its stability or existence."*

The exercise in this booklet titled "Looking for Patterns in Citizen Participation" contains an example of cooptation. The first scenario describes how an outspoken leader was absorbed into the power structure by accepting a paid job.

Cooptation doesn't mean only that an agency puts a community leader onto a board or into an office in order to keep her quiet. It might mean that the leader gets "brought into the fold," helped to understand the "true nature" of the social problems which are occurring, helped to see things from the agency's perspective. (There are, of course, "good reasons" why "we" do things the way we do.) Thinking in that vein, others have redefined and broadened Selznick's concept of cooptation:

> "Cooptation is the process through which an organization succeeds in defining problems which appear to threaten its stability or existence in such a way that the actual resolution of the problems will be amenable to its continued stability or existence."**

The article which follows, although written with tongue in cheek, is a serious example of this broader type of cooptation. Lord North doesn't try to hire Mr. Jefferson or put him on a committee (though he does treat him, as the submitter of a funding proposal, in a potentially subservient relationship). What Lord North does is to define the problems in a way which is more amenable to the continued stability or existence of the colonies, rather than as a declaration of independence.

---

* Philip Selznick, **TVA and the Grassroots**, p. 13.
** Roland Warren and others, **The structure of Urban Reform**, p. 56.

Is This Any Way to Start a Revolution?

by Edward Schwartz

Recently I was asked to write a grant proposal for a project in Pennsylvania related to adult education. After accepting the offer I discovered that the guidelines for this proposal had to conform to federal specifications. I did endure this remarkable procedure, but shortly thereafter conjured in a horrible nightmare the following letter written to Thomas Jefferson in late July 1776.

July 20, 1776

Mr. Thomas Jefferson
Continental Congress
Independence Hall
Philadelphia, Pa.

Dear Mr. Jefferson:

We have read your "Declaration of Independence" with great interest. Certainly, it represents a considerable undertaking, and many of your statements do merit serious consideration. Unfortunately, the Declaration as a whole fails to meet recently adopted specifications for proposals to the Crown, so we must return the document to you for further refinement. The questions which follow might assist you in your process of revision.

1. In your opening paragraph you use the phrase "the Laws of Nature and Nature's God." What are these laws? In what way are they the criteria on which you base your central arguments? Please document with citations from the recent literature.

2. In the same paragraph you refer to the "opinions of mankind." Whose polling data are you using? Without specific evidence, it seems to us, the "opinions of mankind" are a matter of opinion.

3. You hold certain truths to be "self-evident." Could you please elaborate. If they are as evident as you claim, then it should not be difficult for you to locate the appropriate supporting statistics.

4. "Life, liberty, and the pursuit of happiness" seem to be the goals of your proposal. These are not measurable goals. If you were to say that "among these is the ability to sustain an average life expectancy in six of the 13 colonies of

---

This article originally appeared as "Letter from Lord North to Thomas Jefferson," by Edward Schwartz. **Social Policy**, July-August, 1974, pp. 10-11. Copyright 1974 by Social Policy Corporation, New York, New York 10036. Reprinted by permission.

at least 55 years, and to enable all newspapers in the colonies to print news without outside interference, and to raise the average income of the colonists by 10 percent in the next 10 years," these would be measurable goals. Please clarify.

    5. You state that "whenever any Form of Government becomes destructive of these ends, it is the Right of the People to alter or to abolish it, and to institute a new Government. . . ." Have you weighed this assertion against all the alternatives? Or is it predicated solely on the baser instincts?

    6. Your description of the existing situation is quite extensive. Such a long list of grievances should precede the statement of goals, not follow it.

    7. Your strategy for achieving your goal is not developed at all. You state that the colonies "ought to be Free and Independent States," and that they are "Absolved from All Allegiance to the British Crown." Who or what must change to achieve this objective? In what way must they change? What resistance must you overcome to achieve the change? What specific steps will you take to overcome the resistance? How long will it take? We have found that a little foresight in these areas helps to prevent careless errors later on.

    8. Who among the list of signatories will be responsible for implementing your strategy? Who conceived it? Who provided the theoretical research? Who will constitute the advisory committee? Please submit an organizational chart.

    9. You must include an evaluation design. We have been requiring this since Queen Anne's War.

    10. What impact will your program have? Your failure to include any assessment of this inspires little confidence in the long-range prospects of your undertaking.

    11. Please submit a PERT diagram, an activity chart, and an itemized budget.

    We hope that these comments prove useful in revising your 'Declaration of Independence."

Best Wishes,

Lord North

Edward Schwartz is President of the Institute for the Study of Civic Values.

The Power Broker

by Robert Caro

It's not uncommon for a citizen group to run up against unresponsiveness, secretiveness and manipulation on the part of government officials. The Watergate years certainly made that clear. But Richard Nixon did not invent manipulation. Consider the case of Robert Moses, former parks commissioner for the City of New York, and the director of the Triborough Authority. In the mid-1930s, Moses was aggressively developing the Henry Hudson Parkway, which was to run through Riverside Park on the west side of Manhattan. When he came to the northwest corner of Manhattan, Moses chose a route that was unpopular with local residents. Robert Caro, in his book, **The Power Broker**, offers an explanation of Moses' strategy for dealing with the residents:

> Moses' reluctance to discuss his plans for the northern section of the West Side Improvement was understandable. He could not, after all, tell Exton and Weinberg [community leaders] the real reasons he wanted the approach to the Henry Hudson Bridge to be through Inwood Hill Park instead of along the street at its edge: if word ever leaked out that a six-lane highway was being classified as a "park access road," the CWA and WPA would have to reclassify the project. Moses could not explain to Exton and Weinberg that while it might be better to build the bridge on a lower level near the existing drawbridge and therefore avoid Inwood Hill Park and Spuyten Duyvil, his idea of the proper location didn't matter; only the bankers' ideas mattered because it was the bankers who had to put up the money for the bridge. Moses could not, in fact, allow any discussion of the bridge location at all, because discussion generates controversy, and controversy frightens away the timid, and no one is more timid than a banker where his money is concerned. "The market was so skittish that any little thing could have gotten them to back out," Jack Madigan recalls. "A lesser fellow wouldn't have understood the importance of killing off this agitation right at the start before it began raising up some publicity and getting people arguing," but Moses understood perfectly. The financing of the Northern section of the West Side Improvement had been made possible only by the remarkable ingenuity on Moses' part, an ingenuity that bent rules and regulations - twisted them, in fact, until they were all but unrecognizable - into a shape that permitted the participation in the financing of the project of bankers and 22 separate city, state and federal agencies. Exposure of that ingenuity to the public would tumble in an instant the house of cards he had so laboriously erected. He could not allow it.
>
> And what good would discussion do anyway? The city had been trying to build the West Side Improvement for decades - generations, in fact. It had never, even in the free-spending Walkerian era, been able to find the funds to do the job. It could only be done now because of the Federal Relief Program - and that program might be curtailed at any time. If the job was ever to be done, it had to be done at once, without delay. Discussion meant delay, and therefore discussion could not be permitted. "There was no alternative, see - no alternative," Madigan says.

The Power Broker, by Robert Caro. pages 560-561. Copyright 1974 by Alfred A. Knopf, Inc. Used by permission.

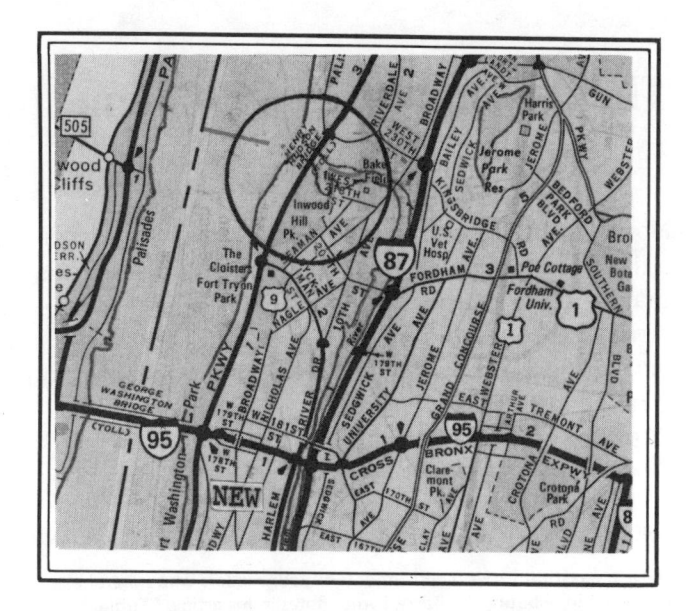

> Madigan's statement was not accurate. There was an alternative—it just was not an alternative that he, or Robert Moses, would even consider. There might be no alternative if the bridge had to be built immediately, but why did it have to be built immediately? If the bankers refused to finance its construction unless it was located on the escarpment, a location which required the destruction of Inwood Hill Park and Spuyten Duyvil, why was it necessary to accept their terms? The city could simply refuse them and wait until it could build the bridge itself, in the place where it should be built.
>
> But the bridge was built, and in order to minimize opportunities for community opposition Moses displayed his skill at rapid construction.
>
> The speed with which the West Side Improvement was driven to completion was symbolized by the construction of the bridge that carried the Henry Hudson Parkway over Broadway at 253rd Street in Riverdale, a job that would normally have taken at least a year to complete. The legislation authorizing construction of the bridge (by the State Council of Parks) was signed at 1:00 p.m., May 1, 1935. At 5:00 p.m. that same day Moses opened bids on the job and let the contract; at 7:00 am the next morning, laborers were working on the site; 12:00 midnight a few weeks later, while most Riverdalians were asleep, the seven-foot-wide steel spans that would hold the road bed of the bridge rumbled up Broadway on huge flat floats pulled by tractors and at 5:55 a.m., the last rivet securing them in place over Broadway was set; when Riverdalians went to work in the morning there before them was a bridge where none had existed the night before.

The routing of the Parkway chosen by Moses was, according to Robert Caro, a loss in both aesthetic and environmental terms.

Perhaps the worst of it was that the 5,500 park benches installed (by Moses) facing the Hudson River offered a view almost entirely obliterated by the Parkway. The motorists might catch a quick glance of the river's beauty but the pedestrians in the park with the time to enjoy the view were denied it.

Or perhaps the worst of it was that citizens once again experienced the futility of trying to confront manipulative officials and instead had their community shaped by those in positions of economic power.

The Accountability Problem

Not all critics of citizen involvement favor a stronger citizen voice. One of the most frequent objections is that a citizen board does not have the same requirement of accountability (to those whom they represent) as does a formal legislative body. This objection is raised in the following piece which appeared as a letter to the editor of a Canadian newsletter, *Constructive Citizen Participation.**

Dear Sir,

I have a question for you and for any of your readers who might be interested in debating it. Barry Sadler notes in his article "Public participation is still seen as an opportunity for citizens to inform and consult rather than to share in the making of policy." My question is this: **In a democratic society, should 'citizens' have a share in policy making?** Or should policy-making continue to be ultimately the responsibility of the politicians who can be held accountable for these policies?

It strikes me that allowing citizens to share in policy-making, as opposed to consulting citizens and receiving their opinions before deciding on a policy, can lead to a diffusion of responsibility for those policies and would leave those who disagree with such policies unable to hold anyone directly accountable. Consent is desirable but seldom possible when policies are enacted which affect the lives, hearts and pocketbooks of a large number of people.

The buck must stop somewhere, after the citizen has added his two-bits worth. I would prefer to have it stop with someone over whom I have some measure of control.

To anticipate the argument that I could elect a citizen to represent me in policy decision-making, I respond that I already do elect such citizens: i.e., my MP, MLA, municipal councillor, and so forth.

Perhaps there are other arguments I have not anticipated.

Yours truly,

Ms. Cathie Fornssler
Information and Extension Coordinator
Church Hill River Board of Inquiry

The Crisis of Democracy
by Samuel P. Huntington

Another example of skeptical writing about citizen involvement—a much stronger attack on citizen activism—appeared in a 1975 book by Samuel P. Huntington, **The Crisis of Democracy: Report on the Governability of Democracies.** The book takes on special significance because it was sponsored and published by the Trilateral Commission.

The commission, "formed in 1973 by private citizens of western Europe, Japan, and North America," consists largely of financial and industrial magnates as well as academics and politicians. Many of Jimmy Carter's top cabinet and security posts were filled by commission members. A 1975 book written for the commission and titled **The Crisis of Democracy: Report on the Governability of Democracies** contains the following statement by co-author Samuel P. Huntington

> Al Smith once remarked that 'the only cure for the evils of democracy is more democracy.' Our analysis suggests that applying that cure at the present time could well be adding fuel to the flames. Instead, some of the problems of goverance in the United States today stem from an excess of democracy.... Needed, instead, is a greater degree of moderation in democracy.... The effective operation of a democratic political system usually requires some measure of apathy and non-involvement on the part of some individuals and groups.

Huntington goes on to say that every democractic society has had groups that were not very involved in politics. He calls this condition "inherently undemocratic" but helpful in making democracy function effectively. As uninvolved groups become more involved, it will be necessary for all groups to exercise more self-restraint, says Huntington. And then this remarkable paragraph:

> Democracy is more of a threat to itself in the United States than it is in either Europe or Japan where there still exists residual inheritances of traditional and aristocratic values. The absence of such values in the United States produces a lack of balance in society which, in turn, leads to the swing back and forth between creedal passion and creedal passivity. Political authority is never strong in the United States, and it is peculiarly weak during a creedal passion period of intense commitment to democratic and egalitarian ideals. In the United States, the strength of democracy poses a problem for the governability of democracy in a way which is not the case elsewhere.**

The Crisis of Democracy includes an appendix with dissenting viewpoints. Author Huntington, for his part, was appointed by President Carter as coordinator for security planning of the National Security Council.

Discussion Questions:

- *Are there limits to democracy? Are there points where too much self-governance becomes a threat?*

- *How does one identify the opposite problem: too much governmental authority? What would the symptoms be?*

- *Some people hold that all who are affected by a decision should be directly involved in making that decision. Do you agree with that principle? Do you consider it to be in conflict with Huntington's observations?*

---

*Vol. 5, No. 3 (March, 1978) p.2, **Constructive Citizen Participation** is available for $4 per year for students and volunteer leaders; $12 per year for organizations. Development Press, Box 1016, Oakville, Ontario, Canada.

****The Crisis of Democracy**, pp. 113-115.

Issues in Citizen Involvement

There are issues which are repeatedly raised about citizen involvement, issues which you may have to confront in your own effort to be an effective citizen. The first step is to develop a familiarity with the issues, so here is one sample listing for your consideration. The second step is to practice taking stands on issues; the exercises after the list will challenge you to do that.

Participation Dilemmas

1. There are no assurances that the public will be involved in identifying which decisions should have public input.

2. Public involvement cannot avoid the dilemma of manipulating public support by disseminating selective or "tainted" information, winning support by favors and otherwise influencing outcomes.

3. There is no way of knowing whether all interests (both geographic and issue-specific) are represented in making a decision.

4. There is no way of assuring that public input is used in making a decision.

5. Under the present system of public involvement, there is no way of assuring that preferences for alternatives reflect a full understanding of the associated benefits and costs.

6. There is no mechanism for measuring the intensities of preferences expressed by various public interests or for assuring that "the public interest" will be served in decision making.

7. The preferences of various interests are difficult to weigh in making a decision.

8. There is uncertainty about rules or procedures that will be used by agencies in arriving at a decision.

*Abstracted from **Public Land Policy: An Evaluation of Decision and Citizen Involvement Systems,** by David L. Erickson, H.K. Cordell and A. C. Davis, a paper at the Rural Sociology annual meeting, Madison, Wisc., September 1977; and printed in **Constructive Citizen Participation,** Vol. 5, No. 3 (March 1978), p. 2.

Exercise: Taking Stands on Participation Dilemmas

no. people: three to many
min. time: 20 minutes
materials: paper and pencil; copies of "Participation Dilemmas"

Process:

1. Review the list of Participation Dilemmas above, and decide whether you would make additions to it based on your own group's experience, or on what you have observed in your community. List them.

2. Practice taking stands on the Dilemmas, and any other issues you've identified. Do this in the style of a class in improvisational speaking: everyone is assigned one issue and has one minute to plan a three-minute presentation, which they will deliver to the rest of the group. Statements should begin with a restatement of the issue and can continue, "Therefore, what needs to be done is....."

3. Each mini-speech could be followed by a quick round of one-sentence reactions: arguments for the other side, other arguments in support of the speaker, words of praise for a good statement.

4. After all have spoken, the group should consider the questions which follow.

Discussion Questions:

- *Where do these dilemmas come from—who or what causes them?*

- *Who should bear the primary responsibility for resolving these dilemmas— citizens or decision-makers?*

- *What **can** be done about each issue? (If you have done the impromptu speaking in step two above, which answers did you find the most satisfying?)*

- *Do these issues help you identify points at which your citizen group has run into difficulty? Can you think of strategies for becoming more effective based on your reactions to the issues?*

- *What is the single issue that has been most troublesome for your organization?*

What's Not Getting Dealt With?

It has been said that democracy is the most inefficient form of government, that despotism would be much more efficient if we were willing to pay the cost. In our representative democracy, the gears often seem to turn slowly; at the time of this writing, a House Special Committee is investigating the assassination of Dr. Martin Luther King which occurred over a decade ago.

Worse than the issues which get dealt with belatedly are the issues which never get dealt with at all. Often it falls to citizen activists to raise to the public's attention issues of significance which for one reason or another are being avoided by decision makers. Consider some cases in which citizen groups "called a question" to the attention of the decision-makers who had been reluctant to consider an issue:

Vietnam

1. American involvement in the Vietnam war was brought under public scrutiny in large part because of growing opposition to the war by activist citizens. There was resistance by the government to a full public debate on the war in part because years of cover-up would be exposed, including repeated lies and doubletalk by presidents and other high officials. ...It takes persistent citizen efforts to expose the emperor's lack of clothes.

The environment

2. For a factory to eliminate its pollution by installing air and water purifying devices is expensive. Instead, society had been bearing this cost of production with health hazards, spoiled recreational facilities and filth. The producers apparently "hoped we wouldn't notice," but too many citizens did, and in organized groups they insisted that the producers should have to pay for the needed pollution control devices. (Enforcement of the recent environmental protection laws is requiring continuing citizen pressure.) ....It takes citizen pressure to get business to spend extra money to protect the public's well-being.

Runaway shops

3. Especially in the Northeastern United States, many factories are being moved out to areas where labor is cheaper such as the Sunbelt or developing countries. In some cases this has been avoided through the determined efforts of workers and other citizens to preserve their jobs and their communities. (Either the workers and the communities have had to make concessions such as lower wages and taxes, or else the workers have let the company go, bought the plant, and started a worker-controlled corporation.) ...Any time citizens challenge the "freedom" of those with wealth to make the decisions which maximize their profits, they run against the grain of the free enterprise tradition, and have to push very hard to get what's best for their community.

Preservation of petroleum reserves

4. New technologies or changing situations can raise issues which decision-makers often persist in ignoring. Society may choose to take an easy path which has heavy costs for future generations—ignoring the rights and concerns of generations yet unborn. For example, some scientists would advise us that our petroleum reserves had best be held untouched so that future generations will have a source of petro-chemicals (such as plastics), and that we therefore need to turn to other forms of energy immediately rather than exhausting our petroleum reserves first. This is an issue which doesn't have a strong voice of advocacy among citizen groups, and politicians and corporate executives certainly aren't talking about it.

...It takes a strong citizen voice to get society to examine issues for which there is no precedent, or issues for whom the "victims" are not yet born.

Nuclear power

5. It has been citizen groups, and not the Nuclear Regulatory Commission, which have brought the health and safety dangers and the costs of nuclear power to the public's eye. Whenever there are large profits possible, and especially when large sums have already been invested, it is an uphill struggle to bring an issue to a fair hearing.

Often, it seems that government and business manage to miss the boat **most** of the time—that they never deal squarely with the basic hopes and fears of the people. The most persistent example is war. A British statesman put it this way, speaking at the end of World War II:

"There has never been a war yet which, if the facts had been put calmly before the common folk, could not have been prevented. The common man is the greatest protection against war."

—Ernest Bevin
speech delivered to the
House of Commons;
November, 1945

Some people have argued that a politician is inevitably short-sighted because of the need to consider what it takes to get reelected.

Brazilian philosopher-educator Paulo Freire* stresses a different problem—the difficulty we all have grasping the crucial issues of our own times. It's the "fish-in-water" problem; we don't have the historian's advantage of hindsight, so it is a tough job to grasp the underlying essence of our day-to-day concerns, to understand the issues of the day as part of a larger picture.

We think it's important for citizen groups to try to develop a sense of that "big picture"—not so that they will abandon their specific issues, but so they will understand how their own issues connect with those of other people and so that they will not stop short of raising the basic problems and questions which are embedded in their own struggles.

*see Paulo Freire, **Education for Critical Conciousness**.

Movement for a New Society/Diana Davies

The Crucial Issues of Our Times

1) **The issue of size; centralization vs. decentralization.** How big should our governmental units and our corporations (or other production units) be? The trend seems to be toward huge governmental units and toward multinational corporations with gross receipts larger than many nations' GNPs. What gets lost in this process? Which forms of technology and social organization lend themselves to smaller units? Are smaller units always more humane?

2) **The boundary between public and private control, between the political and economic spheres.** Will government take over, regulate, or stand back from industries and services ranging from health care to energy production to materials production (steel, mining, etc.) to consumer goods production? What political-economic system will be most capable of coping with environmental problems, resource shortages, changing technologies, worker dissatisfaction?

3) **Nationalism vs. Globalism.** Will we see the world as separate countries increasingly divided by competition over resources and by demands of the have-nots for a piece of the pie, or as a global society, mutually interdependent, needing to succeed together at the risk of global calamity?

4) **Human liberation vs. Racism, classism, sexism, ageism.** Will each human being have the opportunity to work toward his or her potential, or will long-standing barriers of prejudice and discrimination continue? Will progressive trends regarding the role of women continue or be reversed? What about the persistent discrimination and oppression of the young, the old, and the lower classes? Can racial oppression be terminated in southern Africa and elsewhere around the world?

5) **Reactivity vs. Proactivity/Creativity.** Will we become increasingly passive recipients of information and culture, accepting mass media definitions of issues and problems, or will we become definers of reality, proponents of issues, creators of culture?

Discussion Questions

- *What issues in your community are not getting raised? What could citizen groups do to bring them to public attention?*

- *What are the crucial themes in your personal life? Your hopes and fears? Your ambitions and things you hope to accomplish?*

- *What do you consider to be the crucial issues of our times? What issues would you add to or subtract from the list above?*

- *Consider the specific goal or issue of your citizen group. How is it linked to the crucial issues of our times?*

- *What changes might you make in the work of your citizen group, or in your personal life, based on the answers you have just given?*

Forum/cpf

Options and Obstacles

The Forms of Citizen Participation

When you're trying to evaluate existing citizen participation efforts (or to plan a new one), it's helpful to have a sense of the options. A lot of different forms or mechanisms have been tried. The table which follows briefly compares most of the current ones. It is difficult to present comprehensive, balanced information or evaluations in the limited space available. Activities later in this manual call on you to develop your own evaluations of those mechanisms which may be useful models for your group.

Since the list of mechanisms is long, it is divided into five main categories.

1. **Government-Initiated Mechanisms**
   - 1A. Mechanisms Related to Elections
   - 1B. Mechanisms Related to the Legislative Process
   - 1C. Mechanisms of One-Way Communication from an Executive Agency
   - 1D. Temporary or Permanent Convenings
   - 1E. Methods for Assessing Public Opinion
   - 1F. Mechanisms for Decentralization and Grievance-Processing
   - 1G. Support Mechanisms for Citizen Groups
   - 1H. Non-Mechanisms

2. **Future-Oriented Mechanisms**
   - 2A. Information-Age Techniques
   - 2B. Planning Techniques

3. **Citizen Participation in Private Agencies**

4. **Citizen Participation in the Economic Sphere**

5. **Citizen-Initiated Mechanisms**
   - 5A. Citizen Organizations
   - 5B. Citizen-group Strategies
   - 5C. Temporary convenings
   - 5D. Coalitions
   - 5E. Demonstration Projects and Alternative Institutions

1. Government-Initiated Mechanisms

Most of the mechanisms in this category are initiated by a governmental body—a legislature or executive agency, for example. Some, such as the referendum, may be initiated by citizens (the "initiative petition"), although in that case the mechanism was originally created by legislative action. All of the mechanisms in this category pertain to the operations and the policy-making of some governmental body or another.

1A. Mechanisms Related to Elections

Mechanism	Description/Function	Evaluation
Political Party	Nominates and elects public officials; conduit for campaign funds.	Membership relatively open, but influence may depend on years of involvement, wealth, etc.
Voting for Candidates for Public Office	Open to all registered voters; selection of public officials according to information provided during campaign (and, for incumbents' past performance).	Those elected don't necesarily see themselves as accountable to platforms or to voters. Elections are generally held only once or less per year.
Referendum on an issue	Popular vote on a measure proposed by legislative body or by citizens.	Voters can express opinions on specific issues; votes depend on information available and corporations sometimes invest large sums to promote their position through the media.

1B. Mechanisms Related to the Legislative Process

Most citizen participation forms have developed around the executive functions of government (including the various specialized agencies), but there are certain forms which pertain to the legislative and judicial branches.

Mechanism	Description/Function	Evaluation
Legislative Advisory Committee	Provides information to legislators which becomes the basis for drafting or revising legislation.	Generally limited to a small number of articulate citizens.
Legislative Hearings	Opportunity for interested parties to provide formal testimony on matters being considered for legislation.	Same as above.

Jury Duty	Supposedly random selection of citizens to serve a crucial role in the administration of justice.	Bias is introduced by granting of releases and by selection process.
Town Meeting	In some communities, allows all registered voters to approve local budget, reallocate funds, appoint committees, etc. The representative town meeting (a large body of elected representatives) is increasingly common in towns which once had direct town meetings.	Usually meets only once per year.
Class Action Litigation	One or a few citizens can seek to redress a grievance on behalf of a group of other citizens in the same situation.	Has made it feasible to bring to court grievances which may be minor to any one individual but which constitute a significant problem to the group or class.

1C. Mechanisms of One-Way Communication from an Executive Agency

Many mechanisms related to the executive branch of government will be viewed cautiously because they are mechanisms of communication in one direction: from the government to the people.

Mechanism	Description/Function	Evaluation
Open Meetings	Meetings held in open session, available to the public for observation, not participation. (Distinct from "Public Meeting," which will follow.)	Provides information about governmental process, but not citizen input. Not a total guarantee against back-room deals and secret influences.
Document Access	Public access to all government documents (with crucial exceptions to protect individual privacy or national security) is now required by law.	Has provided the basis for numerous citizen-initiated reforms.
Citizen-Language Documents ("translations" from technical or legal language)	The Carter administration issued a lengthy memorandum in the spring of 1978 urging all departments to simplify the language of their documents to allow for maximum public understanding.	"Translation" of technical materials is time-consuming and therefore costly. It is not done consistently and, when done, it is not necessarily done well.
Public Information Campaigns	Use of mass media or other channels by an agency to provide information about proposed programs (and services available) to relevant segments of the public.	Information can provide the basis for citizen input. However, an information campaign alone can represent an attempt to persuade rather than involve the public.

1D. Temporary or Permanent Convenings

Temporary or permanent convenings of citizens monitor the programs and projects of an agency.

Mechanisms	Description/Function	Evaluation
Temporary Convennings, limited size • Task Force • Blue Ribbon Panel	Opportunity to make recommendations to government agency.	Limited number of participants; usually selected by agency. Biased toward articulate elite. Temporary; may not be in existence at the best moment to influence decision-making.
Comment Solicitation	Similar to above, but without face-to face meeting. Citizens or organizations receive copy of bill, regulation, or project plan for comment.	May be open to any interested citizen with access to documents through public libraries. Promotes individual response directed to agency, rather than any organized response from concerned citizens.
Temporary Convenings unlimited size • Public Hearings • Public Meetings • Public Briefings	Opportunity for citizens to recieve information on a specific issue, to ask questions and, at times, to express opinions. Attendance open; mass media or posters used to publicize.	No guarantee that citizens' ideas will be used even if they are received. Information presented may be biased or incomplete. Controversies may be minimized or avoided. Attendance often poor.
Impact Review Process	The National Environmental Protection Act of 1970 (NEPA) requires citizen participation in the review of economic, social, and environmental impacts of federally-funded construction projects. Many states have similar acts. Citizen participation generally incorporates various mechanisms, including public meetings and hearings, solicitation of comments, information campaigns and occasional workshops.	See evaluation of specific mechanisms. NEPA's requirements have produced one of the most far-reaching citizen involvement activities. The publication of information about impacts has influenced some decisions before they were made, and has provided the basis for class action suits in the courts. However, many feel that citizen involvement under NEPA is often too little, too late, because agencies sometimes have their minds made up before they see citizen input or the result of impact studies.

Continuing Mechanisms • Mandated boards or councils • Advisory boards • Commissions • Authorities	Ongoing structures created by legislative mandate or executive order. Some appointed, some elected. May report to a chief executive (governor, mayor) or to an agency. Local as well as state examples include Planning Commissions, School Boards, etc.	Often isolated from real decision-makers, with no guarantee that recommendations will be acknowledged, much less heeded. Does provide opportunity for participants to become knowledgeable, but at the price of broader participation by those not able to accept long-term membership.
Review Board	Citizen review of policy, program, and/or budget of an agency. Often occurs on the regional level. May or may not have more influence than the other continuing mechanisms above.	Review of policy and budget can provide an opportunity for the citizen group to be especially influential. As with the other forms, a "citizen group" may turn out to have a majority of service providers or people with vested interests, and only a minority of citizens at large.
Citizen Representatives on policy-making bodies	Occasionally citizens will be asked to serve on decision-making bodies of various types. (They may go by some of the names listed above.) In these cases the citizens-at-large are in a minority, with elected or appointed officials in the majority.	A limited number of citizens is unlikely to represent the full range of citizen opinion. Cooptation of key citizen leaders by appointment to such a body is not uncommon.

1E. Methods for Assessing Public Opinion

As a group, mechanisms for assessing citizen opinion tend to treat the citizen as an isolated individual and to solicit a passive reaction rather than active and creative participation. Perhaps their greatest shortcoming is that the agency, not the citizen, formulates the questions.

Mechanism	Description/Function	Evaluation
Surveys	Gather opinions about program options or past performance. Also, collect information about needs and demographic characteristics of a region.	Can serve an educational function for citizens if data are tabulated and and made available. Can be "busy work" which results in no real or significant changes.
Vouchers	A "dollar vote" of preference for one program over another. Citizens are given vouchers equal to the cost of a service (such as education) and are able to spend it at whatever agency or institution they choose.	Experiments have met with mixed reviews. Educational vouchers have been used not as assurance of equal opportunity and choice for the poor, but as a way for the rich to retrieve their school taxes for use at expensive private schools which the poor cannot afford even with vouchers.

1F. Mechanisms for Decentralization and Grievance-Processing

The two techniques in this group do not involve citizens, but they may succeed in bringing the government closer to the people by making government officials more accessible to citizens.

Mechanism	Description/Function	Evaluation
Decentralization Mechanisms • Field Officers • Branch Service facilities • Little City Halls	Agency representatives or social service providers are geographically closer to those they serve.	No guarantee of actual participation, especially in policy decisions. Depends on attitudes of agencies and of personnel. Potential basis for two-way information flow, but may leave citizens in passive role.
Grievance-Processing Mechanisms • Ombudsperson • Public Interest Advocate (e.g., Consumer Advocate)	Investigates citizen complaints about government, about consumer practices, about application of legislation, etc. May act as mediator. Appointed by chief executive agency or legislature.	Potential for increasing accountability of government. Powers often not clearly defined so there may be limits on the type of complaints received or responded to.

1G. Support Mechanisms for Citizen Groups

The ways in which government agencies may support the efforts of citizen groups do not constitute citizen participation in themselves. They should not be confused with participation but they can at times contribute to the success of citizen group efforts.

Support Mechanisms	Description/Function	Evaluation
Training	Workshops, printed materials, or other forms of training provided by agency staff or outside consultants.	Can provide basis for independent citizen activity, or may be manipulative — possible indoctrination to agency viewpoint under the guise of training.
Technical Assistance	Funds for consultants or staff time provided to a citizen group to help it develop its own set of proposals or to review the agency's plans more competently.	Same as for training.
Citizen Honoraria	Stipends or travel allowances to citizen board members as compensation for their time and/or expenses.	May be necessary to insure balanced participation by economically disadvantaged, who otherwise might avoid participation because of travel or child-care expenses. May create a feeling of indebtedness to the agency.

1H. Non-Mechanisms

Volunteering and citizen employment are sometimes included on lists of citizen involvement mechanisms. They are listed here as "non-mechanisms" because they are not designed to involve citizens in decision-making on public policy issues. They are included for contrast with the participation mechanisms.

Non-Mechanism	Description/Function	Evaluation
Volunteering	Unpaid work in local schools, hospitals, or other services. Also, stipended work such as VISTA, Peace Corps, etc.	In general, puts the citizen in the role of service provider without significant input into policy or program planning. Thus, it is not generally a means of citizen involvement in public policy. Familiarity gained while serving as a volunteer may provide the basis for later participation in decision-making.
Citizen Employment	"New Careers" for "paraprofessionals" in the schools, in social services, and elsewhere became a popular approach to the development of career ladders for low-income citizens during the mid-60's. The Comprehensive Employment Training Act (CETA) is a current variation on this theme. Occasionally these programs have allowed citizens to work in a paid capacity on planning or policy matters.	A salary for participation in policy or planning may be the critical element which makes possible a more intensive involvement than otherwise. However, it may be that "he who pays the piper names the tune" and that citizens are not truly free to follow their interests.

IF YOU THINK YOU CAN'T FIGHT CITY HALL, MAYBE NO ONE EVER TAUGHT YOU HOW...

2. Future-Oriented Mechanisms

"Information-Age Techniques" are futuristic in their technology; they utilize electronics hardware or other means which are not generally available today. "Planning Techniques" are future-oriented in their content; they are ways in which citizens can become involved in thinking about the future of their communities, their country, the world, and also of themselves and their families. Both Information-Age and Planning Techniques could be initiated by a governmental body, a grass-roots citizen group or some other organization.

2A. Information-Age Techniques

Although these techniques are not in widespread use today, all have been demonstrated already and some have been demonstrated extensively. The potential usefulness of these techniques must be carefully weighed against the possibility that they may exclude—or even be used to exclude—those who neither comprehend nor have access to these techniques and the electronics hardware which some of them require. If any of these techniques do become common, it will be important to provide training which makes them more accessible to disadvantaged and minority groups.

Mechanism	Description/Function	Evaluation
Interactive Cable TV	Two-way communications on public issues, with information provided to the public or a cable TV station and responses to public issues made via a numbered keyboard in the home.	Opportunity for much greater ongoing participation in policy questions. Audience will be biased according to the sophistication and interest of the programs. A mechanism should be developed whereby citizens could participate in framing the options rather than just reacting to them. Also, such indirect participation should not exclude face-to-face meetings.
Issue Ballots	A variation on the preceding technique, using available technology. Information is provided over TV, radio, and/or newspapers. Ballots are printed in newspapers or are available at some convenient location (Post Office, banks).	Similar to preceding.
Games and Simulations	Simulated decision-making about land use, pollution control, or economic development. Some are computer-assisted: decisions and hypothetical facts are fed into a computer which generates data for another round of decision-making.	Provides information on "human factors" which a planner cannot easily foresee. Provides a more realistic basis for statements about the future than simple extrapolation. Participation generally by an educated few. Can be expensive. No guarantee that recommendations will be heeded in real life.

Teleconferencing and Computer Conferencing	Conferencing among people in remote locations, assisted by television or computer. Computer conferencing can be integrated with computer data retrieval and the same display screens used for both types of information.	Considerably more expensive than telephone conference calls, with the possible exception of data-phone communication between two personal computers as a way of transmitting messages between their operators. These technologies are more likely to be used by business and military decision-makers than by citizen groups. Telephone conferences between a legislator and an auditorium full of constituents is an affordable option, however.
Interactive Graphics	Computer-assisted planning of physical objects using a TV-like display. Used by industry to design lens systems, rockets, cars, etc. Possible use by citizens in land use planning.	Potential for involving citizens in complex planning processes by programming the steps of the process into the computer and providing needed background information. Danger of slanting the process or the information to repeat the planner's preferences or mistakes. Also, biased against citizens who are intimidated by computers, or who don't have access to them.
Value Analysis	A computer-assisted technique for understanding why a group of people prefer certain options (e.g., airport locations or recreation master plans) over others..	May provide a useful basis for generating new options. May "mystify" citizen preferences and provide a basis for arguing for "just about anything."
Situation Rooms	Computer-assisted displays of local or regional information useful to planners. Social as well as physical planning data could be included.	Professional planners with the time to "learn the system" could make much better use of it than citizens. The problem is determining whose assumptions about the nature of social problems will be used to select the data.

| Community Information Displays | Museum-type displays on social issues provide a lower-cost alternative to the situation room above. Commercially-produced displays are still expensive. Homemade displays by many organizations representing many viewpoints are to be preferred. Possible locations: city halls, libraries, shopping malls. | Potential to provide important information and a range of viewpoints. The limits of the medium may be bothersome, but additional information can be provided through brochures, etc. |

2B. Planning Techniques

These mechanisms are directed toward long-range comprehensive community planning.

Mechanism	Description/Function	Evaluation
Planning Workshop	Citizens, assisted by agency planners or technical experts, develop their own plans for land use, social service, etc. May incorporate gaming, simulation, role play, mapping, goal-setting, problem-solving and other techniques.	Citizens initiate plans based on their own values and creativity rather than reacting to plans developed by agency.
Community Planning Centers	Simplified version of simulation room; a storefront or other location where citizens can develop plans, examine maps and other data. An ongoing planning workshop. Could be located with a community information/resource center.	Similar to above. Allows for more people's participation than a temporary event, but may require publicity and "special events" to generate ongoing interest.

LOCAL GROWTH POLICY QUESTIONNAIRE   PAGE 13

2:26 Description of "DESIRED Future": Given the range of things which could happen, what would you like to see in terms of your community's future growth, development, and change? (We will call this the "desired future" for your community.) In particular, how is this different from the "most likely future" described above (see question 2:4)?

Goal Development Programs	Community-wide program, temporary or permanent, for the development of long-range goals for the community.	Opportunity for creative, long-range, integrated thinking about the community's future. Potential for domination by groups which develop an active role or by those who enjoy thinking in long-range, comprehensive terms.
Charette	An intensive planning exercise involving (usually) a cross-section of those interested in or affected by issue. An extended planning workshop.	May provoke constructive new solutions. Many citizens may be unable to devote the extended time generally required (2-10 days). Success usually depends on the quality of the specific group planning techniques.
"Tomorrow" and "2000" Projects	Many states and cities have instituted temporary or ongoing projects to develop comprehensive plans or policy guidelines for the next 25 years. Many incorporate planning workshops or charettes, community-wide issue ballotting, etc. Outcomes stated in terms of desired policies or comparison between a likely scenario for the year 2000 and a more desirable one based on new policies.	Challenges participants to think creatively and comprehensively about the future. Opportunity to identify and work toward ideals rather than settling for minor changes on the grounds that they are feasible at present. However, success in implementation may rest on persuading politicians and other decision-makers that plans have merit.

LOCAL GROWTH POLICY QUESTIONNAIRE   PAGE 14

2:28 Actions Necessary to Achieve "DESIRED Future": What kinds of actions would be necessary in order to encourage the future growth, development, and change of your community to more closely resemble the "desired future"? By whom? What would it take (e.g., money, land, new laws, etc.)? In particular, differentiate between actions by the community and actions by others.

—Massachusetts Local Growth Policy Questionnaire, Office of State Planning, 1976

3. Citizen Participation in Private Agencies

Hospitals, mental health centers and providers of services to specific groups (elderly, retarded, handicapped) often have citizen participation activities. They may institute a citizen involvement component for any of a variety of reasons:

- Federal guidelines—requirements which must be met in order for the agency to receive federal funding

- A desire for prestige, or perhaps the advantage in fund raising, when important people can be listed as members of the board and called upon to help

- An effort to take advantage of local talent and community resources, to expand the agency's services without increasing costs

- Local pressure to be responsive to clients or to the surrounding area

- A desire to anticipate disagreement by having it represented early in board or committee meetings

- A sincere desire to base policy decisions on the advice of a broad cross-section of clients and citizens

Mechanism	Description/Function
Private Agency Citizen Participation	The forms which private agency participation can take include many of those listed already for public agencies, especially the temporary and on-going convenings (hearings, public meetings, advisory boards)

"This is the part of capitalism I hate."
Drawing by Joe Mirachi; © 1965
The New Yorker Magazine, Inc.

4. Citizen Participation in the Economic Sphere

The so-called private sector—profit-making businesses and industries—are not always included in discussions of citizen participation. However, because corporate executives and boards of directors make decisions which affect the lives of all of us, and because there are citizen participation mechanisms which focus specifically on the economic sphere, it seems important to include them. In addition, multi-national corporations have economic and often political power comparable to that of many nations. Corporations use some of the mechanisms listed under section 1 ("Government-Initiated Mechanisms") such as Public Information Campaigns and opinion surveys for assessing public attitudes. These methods may be used, respectively, to publicize a corporation's pollution control measures and social responsibility in job training and hiring practices or to study community satisfaction with corporate policies. Citizens may utilize some of the citizen-initiated mechanisms described in section 5 as they try to influence corporations. Media campaigns and direct action strategies are especially relevant. Also, citizen lobbying can promote new government regulation of the private sector.

Mechanism	Description/Function	Evaluation
Citizen Representatives on Corporate Boards of Directors	Citizen, community or consumer voice on boards of directors, generally with voting rights equal to those of the directors representing stockholder interests.	May stimulate change, but is more likely to be token representation without a significant effect. Allows the corporation to say that citizen interests are being represented. A satisfactory selection process is difficult to establish.

Boycotts	Refusal to purchase the goods of a particular company (or country). Often combined with a campaign of letters from citizen/consumers, explaining their reasons for boycotting, which may include concern for workers (the grape and lettuce boycotts) or opposition to defense contracts (the Dow Chemical boycott during the Vietnam era).	A drop in sales of a few percent can be influential because it cuts the company's profit margin. Most effective when combined with a negotiation process which promotes positive alternatives to the policies being opposed.
Marketing Cooperatives	Small scale producers (such as small farmers) buy supplies and sell goods cooperatively.	Allows the individual citizen to participate in the economic sphere and to be competitive with the large-scale producers.
Consumer Cooperatives	Food cooperatives and other consumer cooperatives provide an alternative to buying from large-scale businesses for any consumer willing to share in the work and the inventory costs of the operation.	The policy-makers for the cooperative are the citizen-members who have opted to participate in the cooperative.

```
┌─────────────────────────────────────────────────────────┐
│              I SUPPORT THE                              │
│   [bell]    BOYCOTT OF J.P. STEVENS PRODUCTS            │
│  FREEDOM                                                │
│   AND      I PLEDGE THAT MY CONSUMER DOLLARS            │
│  JUSTICE                      WILL NOT SUPPORT          │
│    FOR                                                  │
│ J.P. STEVENS  • DISREGARD FOR HEALTH OF WORKERS         │
│  WORKERS      • DISCRIMINATION AGAINST WOMEN            │
│               • RACIAL DISCRIMINATION                   │
│               • CORPORATE LAWBREAKERS                   │
│               • SUB-STANDARD WAGES                      │
│               • SUB-STANDARD WORKING CONDITIONS         │
│                                                         │
│   Signed_____ │
│   Address_____ │
└─────────────────────────────────────────────────────────┘
```

Worker-Controlled Corporations	Worker control—usually accompanied by worker ownership—of a factory has been tried successfully in this country and in England, Sweden, and Yugoslavia, among others. Proponents argue that it extends the principle of democratic self-government to the workplace. Often it has been tried out of economic necessity, such as when a corporation chooses to move to a different region or nation and the workers don't want to relocate. Often has strong community support and can be combined with community ownership (see Section 5F).	Worker-controlled factories have been able to compete well in the open market. They have often been ahead of other corporations in considering such factors as benefits, worker safety and community responsibility.

5. Citizen-Initiated Mechanisms

Mechanisms originated through citizen initiatives have relative freedom from influence by another organization and the possibility of greater objectivity. On the other hand, they have even fewer resources than the mandated or government-initiated groups and have no direct access to decision-makers. They are often accused of being unrepresentative and accountable to no one, although it would be more accurate to say that each group's stand is representative of its own membership and is accountable through the process by which members are selected and positions determined.

Citizen-initiated mechanisms inevitably place the citizen in the active role—making decision about what issues to tackle and what stands to adopt—rather than in the role of reacting to governmental initiatives.

5A. Citizen Organizations

Mechanism	Description/Function	Evaluation
Issue Organization	A citizen group organized around a single issue, such as better schools, tax reform, or water pollution control.	Success varies widely depending on ability to analyze problems, propose solutions, find access to decision-makers and maintain interest in the issue. Other skills discussed in this manual are useful here.
Multi-Issue Organization	An organization which addresses housing, health care, jobs, and recreation. May be a neighborhood organization or a coalition.	See Issue Organization above. It becomes especially important within a multi-issue organization to develop a consensus about project priorities.
Neighborhood Organization, Block Club, Community Organization	Membership is determined geographically rather than by interest in a particular issue. May combine social and recreational activities with those of a multi-issue organization. Sometimes created by government initiative.	See issue and multi-issue organizations. Success is also influenced by the degree to which residents identify with the geographical region selected as the organization's boundary.

5B. Citizen-Group Strategies

Many types of group might choose these strategies. If one strategy is the exclusive or predominant method of a group, it may be an appropriate descriptive name for the group, although the name can be restricting if the group decides to change strategies.

Mechanism	Description/Function	Evaluation
Study Group; Research or Action-Research Group	An organization to gather information and/or analyze a particular issue or community. A study group is generally a small, informal group; an action-research group combines its information-gathering with organizing or political action.	Provides an important basis for citizen group action, especially if the group can develop an independent understanding of social problems and their causes.
Citizen Program Evaluation	A citizen group which evaluates the plans and activities of another organization, such as a governmental agency.	Success depends on the relevance of the findings as well as the use to which they are put.
Citizen lobby	An organization for citizens to counter corporate lobbying within a legislative body. May also use legal pressure within the courts to assure enforcement of exist- laws. The Public Interest Research Groups which exist in many states combine citizen lobby methods with research and program evaluation.	Success limited by existence of competing lobbies and by appropriate legislative action as a solution to a particular problem.
Direct Action Organization	Uses various strategies, ranging from community education to petition drives to demonstrations or civil disobedience.	Success depends on appropriateness and power of strategies selected and the number of people involved.
Petition	Formal or informal request for legislation or for change in executive agency procedures.	Relies on weight of public opinion unless some legal requirements (such as number of signatures required for a ballot referendum) can be fulfilled. If a formal petition, limited to registered voters.

5C. Temporary Convenings

The next two mechanisms are temporary convenings initiated by citizens.

Mechanism	Description/Function	Evaluation
Ad hoc Committee	A temporary, informal citizen group organized around a particular issue.	Success depends on strategies chosen and degree of power and influence attained. See issue organization (section 5A, above).

Problem-Solving Conference	A community-wide conference, either open or invitation-only, designed to develop new options or negotiate new solutions to a specific problem. May utilize planning/futures techniques listed earlier. Useful in calling the public's attention to a problem and generating publicity.	Success depends heavily on whether decision-makers participate, and whether they are willing to accept the input of, or negotiate with, the citizens.

5D. Community Information and Education

Citizen groups often try to educate their fellow citizens about an issue.

Mechanism	Description/Function	Evaluation
Community Resource or Information Centers	A citizen-run information service, providing referrals to social services, facts about community problems and possibly assistance in forming an organization to deal with problems. Might be housed at a public library or in a storefront.	In itself, usually does not represent citizen input into public policy, but may stimulate such input. Depends on individual intiative and interest to first use the facility.
Resource Banks	An information bank of individuals' skills, learning interests, social concerns, etc. May be housed at a community resource center to put people with similar concerns in touch with each other.	See preceding list.
Media Campaigns	Use of mass media by a citizen group to promote wide awareness of an issue, to shift opinion or to bring public opinion to bear on decision-makers.	Depends on accuracy or cooperation of media workers, and whether the media chosen convey factual information or merely an exciting story.
Community Schools	Although usually started to provide adult education and to make fuller use of public school facilities, community schools sometimes are a setting for the education of and input by citizens regarding community issues.	Depends on individual initiatives to lead and participate in community affairs courses and on the accuracy of staff estimates of topics of interest.
Conferences and Institutes	These educational forums can also be used to organize citizens concerned about an issue.	Generally attract only committed and more affluent people because of time and expense required.

Consciousness-raising or Liberation Groups	This approach, which became popular in the women's liberation movement, is being used also by men, homosexuals, workers and members of various minority or oppressed groups. The approach is generally used to understand one's personal situation. It is similar in some ways to a study group but usually has more emphasis on personal experience.	Powerful because personal experience of social problems is generally the most motivating factor in stimulating citizen action.

5E. Coalitions

Citizen groups often join forces to support each others' efforts. Sometimes the liaison will acquire a name.

Mechanism	Description	Function
Coalition, Federation, or Alliance	Cooperation of several citizen organizations based on shared interests and needs.	Larger membership and increased resources may increase power. It may also be possible to hire one or more paid staff. Depending on the formality of cooperation, participating groups may have to give up some of their autonomy.

5F. Demonstration Projects and Alternative Institutions

Especially when citizens have found government officials unwilling to act meaningfully on an issue, they have sometimes developed demonstration projects of their own aimed at providing the desired services or problem-solutions.

Mechanism	Description	Function
Citizen-Based Social Services	"Alternative" social services initiated by an issue organization, neighborhood organization or study group. Generally incorporated as a non-profit organization; may receive public or private monies. Usually establishes a distinctive style of service delivery, such as the extensive use of non-professional ("para-professional") workers.	Difficult to start. Often skims off a segment of service clients who are comfortable with the new service's style, without influencing the procedures of established services. May demonstrate the feasibility of different methods.

Community Owned Corporations	Community residents become owners of a new or existing business within their community through purchase of usually low-cost shares. This fresh capital can be used to expand or diversify the business, provide needed community improvements or finance citizen-based social services. Possible structures include cooperatives and community development corporations. Housing acquisition and rehabilitation have been done by community owned corporations in several cities.	When the relevant decision-makers are corporate executives it may be near-impossible to change policies. This option can work well with proper technical assistance and can provide a community with capital resources.
Government in Exile (Shadow Government)	Perhaps the most notable case was the exiled Vichy government of France during the Nazi occupation during World War II. However, citizen groups have set up informal shadow governments to clarify policy options and to specify the consequences of choices other than those being made by the formal government. Similar to citizen program review and to Tomorrow/2000 Projects. Lends itself to media campaigns.	Since a shadow government has no direct power, success depends on the ability to influence decision-makers directly or to mobilize public opinion.
People's Courts	A citizen's judicial branch; a variation on the "shadow government" idea. If citizens are not able to "get a hearing" in any other way, they may be able to publicize an issue by staging an informal trial. One example is the "Russell Tribunal," (organized by philosopher Bertrand Russell, which heard extensive testimony regarding "crimes against humanity" in the Viet Nam War.	May be criticized as a self-created platform for the beliefs of the organizers. However, may provide an opportunity to present detailed facts and arguments, and to demonstrate the possibility of different courses of action. Shortcomings can be mitigated by bringing in testimony from all sides or by taking an open advocacy stance.

Discussion Questions:

- *Identify the mechanism or organizational type of your own citizen group.*

- *What other forms could it take?*

- *What would be the most powerful or effective form to use in addressing the issue which concerns you?*

- *What combination of mechanisms would be most helpful in working toward a society conducive to the full development of all its people?*

- *What would have to happen to change present mechanisms to more powerful and appropriate ones?*

Visions for Citizen Involvement

In the late 1900s, citizen involvement is faced with many possible forms and many thorny issues. The phenomenon of "information overload" makes it difficult for citizens to keep up with technical subjects and seems to some to support our need to depend on "experts." The society is so complex that a supposed solution to one problem may generate many other problems. Many times the decision makers we would like to reach are not public officials but corporate executives who have no direct accountability to the general public. The world is small enough that problems anywhere affect us and large enough that advantaged people, nations or corporations may be tempted to turn their back on the consequences of their decisions for less fortunate people.

In the face of all this, what will citizen involvement look like in the coming decades? What do we want it to look like? The previous section specified many different forms of citizen involvement. This section discusses eleven visions for understanding citizen involvement. They are not all exclusive of each other, but some are very different or even opposite from others. The discussion questions will stimulate individual contemplation or group discussion using this list of visions.

Vision 1: Representative Democracy

The only realistic way to determine the "will of the people" is to hold elections in which voters select representatives to legislatures and high-level executive officers of their government. Those elected are obligated to use surveys, open meetings or other means to stay in touch with voter opinion.

Vision 2: Direct Democracy Through the Communications Revolution

The New England Town Meeting is the only workable model of true democracy. The Communications Age will offer us the opportunity to return to this level of democracy through two-way cable television with a channel that has continuous public meetings and issue balloting. Technologies still to be developed will further increase direct participation.

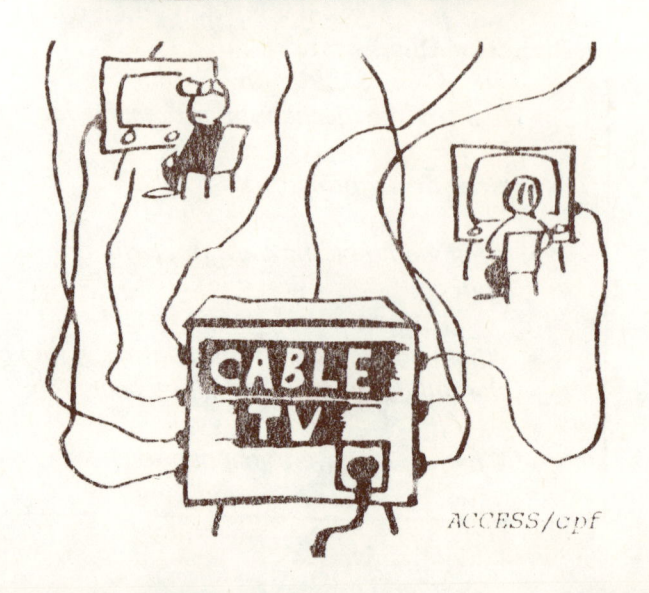

Vision 3: Citizen Boards and Councils

Governments today are so complex and the power of executive agencies is so great that representative democracy must be supplemented by citizen boards and councils, mandated by legislation, to advise or oversee the actions of all major governmental departments. Many citizens would thus be involved in the issues which concern them most. Membership of mandated boards and councils must be representative of the area and members must keep in touch with the views of a cross-section of the public.

Vision 4: Grass-Roots Organizations

Mandated groups are often too close to their agencies to see the problems; they often become preoccupied with reacting to agency plans and programs. Therefore, it's essential to have independent citizen groups which owe their existence to no one but themselves. Independent citizen groups can act as watchdogs on the agencies and hold them accountable, which will balance the effect of corporate lobbyists so that the people have a more equal voice with the monied interests. Also, independent groups can look out for new issues and problems with which governmental bodies aren't yet dealing.

Vision 5: Economic Democracy

A society is not truly democratic unless its economic institutions reflect the values of the workers and the public. We need citizen representatives on corporate boards, and we need to develop mechanisms for worker control and ownership of factories. This more democratic control over both the products and the processes of production may help to reduce workplace health hazards, unsafe products, and environmental damage due to production wastes.

Vision 6: Neighborhood Power

The poverty neighborhoods in all our major cities are symptoms of our inadequate thinking about social problems and our orientation towards promoting wealth and growth rather than direct assault on poverty. The poor support the nation disproportionately through their work and regressive taxes. The only solutions that will work are decentralized solutions. Local neighborhoods need to develop their own industries, sources of power and ways of providing food that will stop the flow of dollars out of the neighborhood. This will require the active participation of many people in community development.

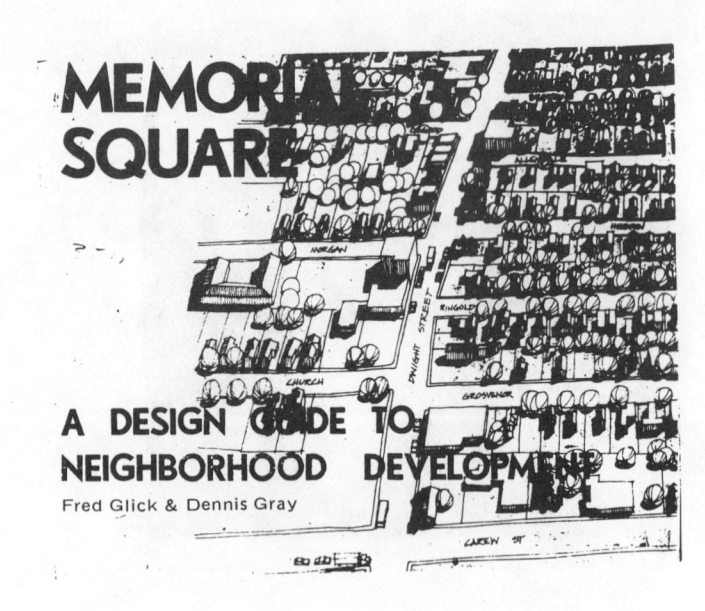

MEMORIAL SQUARE

A DESIGN GUIDE TO NEIGHBORHOOD DEVELOPMENT

Fred Glick & Dennis Gray

Vision 7: Long-Term Concerns

The decisions being made today that look all right for the short run may prove disastrous in the long run. This is especially true in our transition era, marked by the looming exhaustion of oil reserves, the depletion of other important mineral resources and the growth of industrial output to a level that threatens the world's environmental quality. Decision-makers are prone to avoid the long-term implications. Politicians focus their attention on winning re-election in a few years and industrialists plan for short-term profits. Citizen group action must persistently draw attention to the long-term consequences of current decisions out of concern for our futures and as advocates for the disenfranchised, the poor and generations yet unborn who cannot speak for themselves.

Vision 8: Direct Action

There are social problems so entrenched they don't yield to persuasion or petition. Legislatures are slow to act, or legislation is not being implemented. At such times a citizen group may feel compelled to take direct action to correct persistent injustices, as during the Civil Rights movement of the 1960s, or to stop actions which are difficult to reverse, as during the nuclear power demonstrations of the '70s. Boycotts, sit-ins and other means dramatize the problems and attempt to stop them. They are an essential component of powerful citizen involvement.

Bringing about the passage of a new law or pleading cases before the courts of the land does not eliminate the necessity for bringing about the mass dramatization of injustice in front of a city hall. Direct action and legal action complement one another; when skillfully employed, each becomes more effective.

—Martin Luther King

Vision 9: The Silent Majority

There are limits to the amount of citizen pressure and disruption which the social fabric can tolerate. The "silent majority" buffers or softens the impact of the activist minority and helps preserve the integrity of the society.

Vision 10: The Experimental Society

Old solutions are inadequate to the problems of today. The citizens of today and tomorrow will have to take an open, flexible attitude. They must be willing to experiment to find activities that have solved other communities' problems of unemployment, food shortages or rising energy costs.

Vision 11: The Democratic Revolution

Throughout history citizens concerned about just and democratic control of their political and economic institutions have found it necessary to revolt. This, then, is perhaps the most powerful and drastic form of citizen participation. The American Revolution has inspired democratic-minded citizens in many nations to understand that governments and long-standing policies should not be exchanged lightly, that under bearable conditions peaceful solutions should be sought, but that when conditions become insufferable, it is the right and duty of the governed to alter and abolish such governments, even through revolution when it becomes absolutely necessary, and to establish new governments which will ensure the rights of the people.

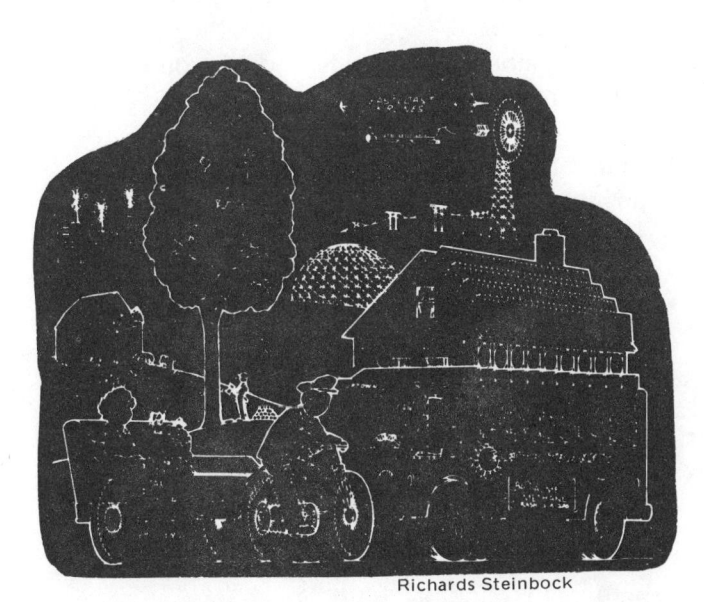

Richards Steinbock

The American War is over; but this is far from the case with the American Revolution. On the contrary, nothing but the first act of the great drama is closed.

— Benjamin Rush, 1787

Discussion Questions:

- Which vision of citizen involvement do you prefer?

- Which vision most resembles the citizen involvement activities that you have been involved in?

- Do you have other visions not described among the eleven?

- Which vision(s) are not compatible with your own? Which would you want to reject?

- Which visions reflect the attitude of decision-makers you come into contact with? Have others role-play such people, and try to persuade them to change to your view.

- Which vision (or combination of visions) offers the most realistic hope for the future?

Diagnosing Your Group's Involvement in Decision-Making

So far, we've talked mostly in terms of citizen participation on a community-wide or even a society-wide basis. Now it's time to focus on one particular citizen group that concerns you—one that you work with regularly, or perhaps one that you're interested in evaluating.

The following questionnaire is really a guided analysis of what's going on within your group.

- Working alone, star any ideas which you think should receive the group's attention.

- In a small group, compare findings and discuss possible courses of action to improve your situation.

- In a large group, take a few items as starting points for discussion.

If you have a set of questions which you would prefer to raise, treat this questionnaire as an example of how to get questions written down in a form which communicates your concerns to others.

"All the powers that be being present and accounted for, let us begin."

Drawing by Dedini; © 1974
The New Yorker Magazine, Inc.

Diagnostic Questionnaire

1. WHO PARTICIPATES?

Citizen involvement efforts have developed to provide a more equal voice for the average citizen in the face of full-time lobbying and campaign contributions by corporations and other monied interests. If some groups are under-represented, "citizen involvement" isn't doing its job.

Check those groups which are involved less than the census would suggest is appropriate. Also groups which should have a special interest in your issue but are, nevertheless, under-represented.

- ( ) white males
- ( ) white females
- ( ) black males
- ( ) black females
- ( ) other minority groups: _____
- ( ) low income people
- ( ) working class people
- ( ) unemployed people
- ( ) people with less than the average level of formal education
- ( ) elders
- ( ) young people (under 18)
- ( ) people who speak English as a second language
- ( ) migrants and other part-time residents
- ( ) people with physical disabilities (blind, deaf, wheelchair-users, etc.)
- ( ) people from all parts of the geographical area involved (specify under-represented areas: _____)
- ( ) people with historically different views on your issue(s)
- ( ) other: _____
- ( ) other: _____
- ( ) other: _____

Place a second check beside the under-represented groups it is most important to recruit. What would you need to do to recruit your targeted groups? What changes would have to be made in your group's goals, strategies or operating style in order to make membership more attractive to those people? How could you find out for sure?

2. ACCESS TO POWER

There are many levels of citizen involvement, varying according to their degree of power. Sherry Arnstein portrayed this range of power as an eight-step ladder (her article is summarized in this manual as a classic analysis of citizen involvement).

Using Arnstein's eight rungs, indicate your group's present level of citizen involvement with a "P." (If you find it hard to rate the group overall, some specific project or attempt at influencing policy may be easier.) Put an "I" next to the ideal level of power where you would like your group to be operating.

_____ 8 Citizen Control (100% citizen decision-making)

_____ 7 Delegated Power (delegated by agency to citizens)

_____ 6 Partnership (power shared between citizens and agency)

_____ 5 Placation (advisory role)

_____ 4 Consultation (inviting opinions)

_____ 3 Informing (one-way information flow, from agency to citizens)

_____ 2 Therapy (involving citizens in planning for the hidden purpose of "curing" their maladjustment, without relinquishing any real power)

_____ 1 Manipulation (engineering support or acquiescence)

How can your group change its level of power?

3. WHO DECIDES?

It's often helpful to pinpoint the ultimate decision-maker for each of the decisions that concern us. Then it becomes helpful to think about how much access (if any) the average citizen and the citizen group have to that decision-maker.

Make a larger version of the table below, copying the sample issues and/or adding others which are concerns of yours. Write in the decision-maker(s), then rate the level of individual citizen access and the level of access which groups achieve (great, moderate, little, none; or note specific events which indicate access or lack of it).

Issue	Who Decides?	Individual Access	Group Access
		.....to decision-maker(s)	
A. Whether to build a new wing on the local hospital.....			
B. Whether to appropriate $2 billion for a new weapons system...			
C. Whether to eliminate special school programs in favor of a "return to basics"...			
D. etc.....			

As another way to understand who decides on a particular issue, you may want to draw a diagram. Write the name of individuals or organizations in circles. Put the decision-maker(s) at the center, with other organizations or individuals near or far from the decision-maker depending on how much influence they seem to have. You could also use arrows of differing thicknesses to show relative influence, and even two-headed arrows if you wanted to show two-way influence. Here is an example of this type of diagram:

Issue: Whether to build a new limited-access connector road between downtown and the interstate highway.

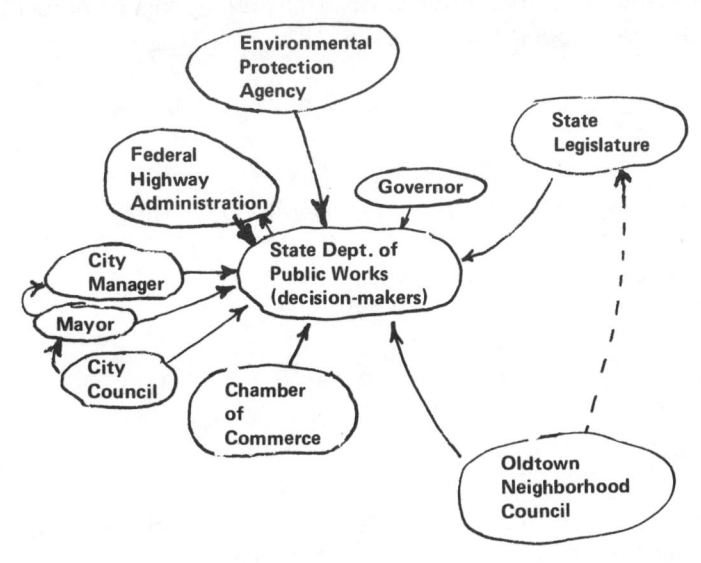

4. AGENCY RELATION TO CITIZEN INVOLVEMENT

If your citizen group works with or attempts to influence a particular government agency, consider its attitude toward citizen involvement. Check the attitude(s) which seem most typical of the agency you relate to.

( ) Citizen involvement as public relations
( ) Citizen involvement as a way to build long-term support for the agency
( ) Citizen involvement as a way to avoid later hostile reaction to projects
( ) Citizen involvement as a source of information on community values and preferences
( ) Citizen involvement as a way to "channel opposition" into acceptable forms
( ) Citizen involvement as a source of new ideas for project design, social service delivery, etc.
( ) Other:_____

5. THE LIMITS OF CHANGE

Sometimes an agency will seem responsive to citizen input until a major request is made; suddenly the citizens find they are speaking to a brick wall. For example, some Vietnam war critics both inside and outside the government found that the questions they raised were beyond what the Congress and the Presidents were willing to discuss. A certain amount of input can be incorporated into "business as usual" but beyond that it is unacceptable.

There have been many explanations offered for this. Some people have argued that professional planners, social service workers and policy makers receive professional training which influences the way they perceive problems; if someone poses a problem outside their professional expertise it threatens their ideas and their jobs. Some argue that a "group-think" phenomenon—a "yes-man" syndrome—can limit the range of ideas an organization finds acceptable. If you can't find anyone who'll listen to your point of view, it may be that someone more politically or economically powerful already has their ears.

- A. What are the "limits" of the agency you encounter most often? What sort of request or demand would they be unwilling to hear or respond to?

- B. Has there been a case in your group's history when you couldn't get a fair hearing? What "limit of change" were you bumping into?

- C. What/Who determines the limits beyond which your agency will not move?

- D. What/Who would it take to change those limits?

6. WHO FRAMES THE QUESTIONS?

Many citizen meetings — whether they're about highways, schools or mental health services — are controlled by the agency personnel who have called the meeting. Even the agendas and mandates of permanent citizen boards are often set by the agencies. So the questions are "Who frames the questions?" and "Who sets the agendas?"

One of the visions for the future of citizen involvement is two-way cable TV with a public issues station presenting issues and raising questions which viewers could vote on by pressing buttons in their homes. But again the problem emerges: "Who frames the questions?" If the question appears on your TV screen: "Should there be tax rebates for people who install more home insulation?" and you advocate solar hot water, you don't have the sort of citizen involvement you'd like to have because you can't amend the question.

- A. Who frames the questions which your group deals with?

- B. Who should frame them?

- C. What could you do to improve things?

- D. What questions should you be asking?

7. WHAT'S ON YOUR AGENDA?

The power of a group is reflected in the type of decisions it can make. If your group is the board of a governmental agency, you may run into resistance if you try to gain more control over the budget, for example. If a board has spent most of its time monitoring the day-to-day administration of a service agency, the agency personnel may be delighted if the board stops "looking over our shoulders" and concerns itself instead with setting basic policy. (That delight may sour if the board starts recommending major changes in service delivery.) A citizen group that has been making only short-term decisions may enhance its influence considerably by shifting to a long-term view. (Agency or corporate decision-makers often have at least a five-year view, and a citizen group needs to do some long-term planning in order to be playing the same game.)

    A.   Does your group have control over its own operating budget?

          ( ) yes   ( ) no

       . . . control or influence over an agency's budget?

          ( ) yes   ( ) no

    B.   How does your group divide its time between . . .

       policy decisions _____%
       administrative decisions _____%

    C.   What is the longest time span which your group considers in making decision?

       _____ years

    D.   Overall, are you dealing with the most important issues? What major issues should be added to your agenda?

8. ANALYSIS

There are differing opinions about how much time a citizen group needs to spend analyzing the underlying causes of the problems that concern it. Most people would agree that it's very valuable to have some agreement on the underlying causes of problems, whether it's as basic as a lack of street lamps or as complex as a shortage of worthwhile jobs.

Many times it is easy to blame an individual for a problem, and to organize against that individual. The politicians put the blame on the poor or the jobless, and vice versa. But the persistent problems are usually based on our systems — the ways we receive health care services, or the ways jobs are created and eliminated in our economic system, for example.

    A.   Does your group spend enough time analyzing the causes of problems?

          ( ) yes   ( ) no

    B.   Would you say that your analysis focuses mostly on . . .

       ( ) individual bureaucrats or politicians
       ( ) individual citizens (e.g., poor, unemployed, . . .)
       ( ) system problems
       ( ) other: _____

    C.   Do your group's analyses of the problems it is dealing with go deep enough to be accurate?

9. BARRIERS TO EFFECTIVENESS

There are some standard pitfalls which are often hard to avoid. At the least, you'll want to know if you've fallen into one.

Is your group trapped . . .

( ) . . . by an agency that seems responsive at public meetings but never does anything?

( ) . . . by not having access to decision-makers?

( ) . . . by not having access to the information you need?

( ) . . . by a lack of needed skills and experience among the members of the group?

( ) . . . by having individuals or the whole group "coopted" into positions that seem powerful and important but don't really lead anywhere?

( ) other: _____

10. DOES IT ALL ADD UP TO PROGRESS?

Sometimes you're doing everything "by the book" and it still doesn't get you anywhere.

A. Is your group getting where it intends to go? Difficulties aside, would you say that your group is doing reasonably well at achieving its goals?

B. What is the most important change you could make to get things back on the right track or to speed your progress?

The dogmas of

the quiet past are inadequate to the stormy present.

— Abraham Lincoln
Second Annual Message to Congress
December 1, 1862

PART II: TAKING ACTION FOR BETTER CITIZEN INVOLVEMENT

Introduction

We hope that the articles and activities in Part I have given you information and experience that are useful in making judgements about citizen involvement programs. Most of all, we hope Part I has given you the courage of your convictions — a trust in your own perception of what's acceptable and what ought to be better.

If you see a need for improvement, what can you do? That's the focus of Part II.

- Do you publicize the shortcomings and lobby for change?

- Do you give up on the existing organizations and start from scratch?

- Do you do your best to develop clout within your organization?

After discussing "how to" ideas for each of these approaches, Part II closes with suggestion for the individual citizen on choosing issues and choosing the organization which can deal with them successfully.

New Structures

A Watchdog Group for Citizen Participation

It is well and good to have a clear analysis of citizen group effectiveness or barriers to it. But that information doesn't help much unless there is some channel or mechanism for bringing opinions and facts to light. One possible mechanism is a watchdog group or council — a government sponsored or independent citizen group whose issue is the quality of citizen involvement.

This approach was proposed in the following Report of the Massachusetts Governor's Commission on Citizen Participation.

A Council for Citizen Participation

It is one thing to enunciate principles of citizen participation; it is another to see them put into effect. This commission does not belive that criteria and suggestions alone will transform state government, but that an enforcement agent is needed. We therefore recommend the establishment of a Council for Citizen Participation.

This Council would be a watchdog agency, advocating and monitoring an increased degree of government "by the people." Its primary tasks would be to audit the citizen participation programs of state agencies, and to scrutinize these agencies to insure that they meet minimum standards for citizen participation. If these standards are not found to be respected, the Council would make recommendations for changes in policy. These tasks could be accomplished through monitoring of selected programs from time to time, and by a thorough annual audit of each agency's overall achievement.

Charges that citizen participation is being preached but not practiced are inevitable: individuals will complain about their treatment at the hand of state officials, citizen councils will contest the limits of their powers, and program workers will quarrel with both councils and officials. The Council for Citizen Participation should act an an ombudsman/arbiter when such differences appear.

The Council could provide a variety of subsidiary services to both private citizens and state officials. Such services might include (1) technical assistance to the secretaries in handling citizen participation efforts, or (2) assistance to citizen groups in the form of duplication, clerical, and mailing help.

The volunteer clearing house recommended in the section on volunteers would be especially effective if attached with adequate funding and staffing to the Council for Citizen Participation. The Council should serve as a highly-visible advocate for volunteers whether it incorporates a volunteer clearing house or not. Visibility, indeed, is vital if the Council is to successfully expand and strengthen opportunities for citizen participation. Located in the Governor's Office, the Council would be sufficiently visible and would have the prestige necessary to give its efforts weight.

The specific powers of enforcement of the Council for Citizen Participation should be precisely defined. They should supplement, not subvert or conflict with, the constitutional prerogatives of the legislative and executive branches. The Council should be concerned primarily with overseeing the effectiveness of basic policy, and with proposing changes in that policy when necessary.

The question of sufficiently funding the Council for Citizen Participation is especially important. Persons with responsibility in the community-care field have described to the Commission their futility and frustration in dealing with insufficiently funded programs.

The Commission does not believe that large appropriations for the Council would be necessary, and it is aware of the necessity for caution in embarking on new state programs. But we also believe that the benefits to be realized by supporting, guiding, and taking advantage of the trend toward greater citizen participation will far outweigh the cost.

The Commission's recommendations for the Council for Citizen Participation are detailed in the proposed legislation which follows.

AN ACT TO ESTABLISH A GOVERNOR'S COUNCIL FOR CITIZEN PARTICIPATION

The following sections shall be added to Chapter 6 of the Massachusetts General Laws as most recently amended: —

Section 1. Definitions. Whenever used in this section and sections the following words shall have the following meanings:

> Citizen participation. Citizen participation shall mean the involvement of any unpaid citizen in the decisions or policies of the Commonwealth or the services and programs thereof.

> Citizen council. Citizen council, a policy-making board established by administrative action or statute to participate in the policies of any particular program of the Commonwealth.

Section 2. There shall be a Council for Citizen Participation in the Office of the Governor, hereinafter called the Council, consisting of three members to be appointed by the Governor and one member of the Senate and one member of the House. The three members appointed by the Governor shall be designated in their original appointments to serve one, two and three years, respectively. Upon expiration of the term of a member or upon his resignation, his successor shall be appointed in like manner for a term of three years. Said members shall serve without compensation but shall receive their expenses necessarily incurred in the performance of their duties. The chairman of the council shall be elected by its members. The council shall meet monthly and at other times at the call of the chairman. At least one such meeting during each year shall be held in each of the following metropolitan areas: Worcester, New Bedford, Springfield, Pittsfield, and Andover. The council shall be provided with suitable quarters in the state house or elsewhere within the Commonwealth. The council shall make an annual report to the General Court and a copy thereof shall be sent to the Governor and the state Secretary. The council may appoint an executive secretary who shall not be subject to Chapter thirty-one, and shall with the approval of the Governor fix his salary. The council may appoint such other assistants, consultants, investigators, and experts as it deems necessary to carry out the provisions of the next section.

Section 3. The council shall audit existing and planned programs for citizen participation. Before such audit reports are published, the council shall assist each Secretary and department head to develop more effective plans for citizen participation. The evaluation by the council of citizen participation in the programs of the Commonwealth shall rely on the following standards:

1. The role of citizen participants shall be clearly defined;

2. The powers and duties so defined shall be sufficient for effective participation;

3. The agency of the Commonwealth shall assign staff and other resources to provide adequate information for the citizen participants to make sound decisions; and

4. The selection process for participation shall include representation of principal interests.

The council shall establish a grievance procedure for citizen councils and individual members thereof to consider complaints regarding their participation.

The council shall promote information exchange, coordination, and cooperation among all existing citizen councils and other forms of citizen participation.

The council shall maintain a service of assistance to citizen groups, including but not limited to, the loan of photographic, reproduction, sound, and other communications equipment.

The council shall promote and monitor implementation of statutes and regulations relating to access to public records.

The council shall promote and monitor the commitment of the Commonwealth to the use of volunteers.

Discussion Questions:

- *Would a watchdog group for better citizen participation be useful in your community/region/state?*

- *What geographical area would be best?*

- *Should it be a government mandated group, or independent?*

- *What steps would be required to get it started? By whom?*

Setting Up a New Citizen Participation Organization (A Planning Guide)

Suppose that you have become concerned about some issue or social problem. You have begun to identify other people who share your concern and want to start a new citizen organization. How can you start off on the right foot, with enough clout to achieve your goals?

This exercise is a "planning guide" — a structured thinking process for you to use as you sit around someone's kitchen table trying to decide what to do first. So take pencil in hand, talk things out as you go, skip sections which don't seem helpful to you, add questions of your own. If there are more than three to five people involved in this planning process, you might break into smaller groups to tackle these questions, then convene the whole group and compare answers.

Part 1: Getting the Right People Involved

Whom do you want to get involved? There are a number of possible and legitimate goals for membership. Check the one which is most appropriate for your group.

( ) Like-minded people interested in advocating a particular position

( ) A diversity of viewpoints to promote dialogue among various positions

( ) A representative cross-section of a community (by race, age, income level or formal education, for example)

( ) 100% of those people affected by an issue

( ) Other: _____

Of course I want to change things. But what can one person do?

— Vocations for Social Change

HOW TO CHOOSE

Once you have identified potential members, you have a guide for recruitment or appointment; it can even help you determine what selection process would be most appropriate.

Here are some options for determining who the members are. Rate your first, second, and third choices by placing numbers 1, 2, and 3 next to them.

_____ Open membership; anyone interested can attend.

_____ Open membership for anyone within a particular geographical area.

_____ Community elections (example: an elected neighborhood council)

_____ Open membership up to a maximum number

_____ Appointed by the agency to which the citizen group relates

_____ Half appointed citizens (appointed by agency); half elected by citizens

_____ Membership restricted to consumers of an agency's services (rather than citizens at large)

_____ One of the above plans (or a combination of several) but with a minimum number of some important group, such as recipients (clients) of a social service, residents of a target neighborhood or people below a certain income level, for example.

_____ Other: _____

Use the 1-2-3 ratings to determine the group's aggregate preferences. If you do not all agree, you may want to make a table similar to the one below that will compare the three most popular options.

Option	Advantages	Disadvantages
open membership		
community elections		
Other: Open, but with elected steering comm.		

Make a version of this table large enough to summarize each member's comments under "Advantages" and "Disadvantages." Then everyone can review the "pros" and "cons" as a basis for a decision. Leave room for new options (perhaps combinations of the top few preferences) generated during your discussion.

WHAT ROLE FOR THE PROFESSIONALS?

What role, if any, should be provided for professionals such as social workers, other helping professionals, engineers or planners? Sympathetic professionals working with a citizen group bring technical expertise and may add weight and credibility to the statements or positions of a citizen group. A group composed entirely of professionals, acting as citizens concerned about a public policy, can be especially influential (for example, scientists or doctors pointing out the dangers of nuclear power).

On the other hand, professionals sometimes have very different concerns and perspectives from the general public. Social service agencies sometimes create "consumer-provider boards" which are half citizens ("consumers" of the social service) and half providers (the social service professionals who provide the service). The providers may argue for higher pay, standardized procedures (rather than individualized treatment) and other changes which would do more to benefit providers than consumers. This adversary situation doesn't always develop, and the consumer-provider board does provide the opportunity for interaction between the two groups. However, the combined board structure may prevent consumers (citizens) from developing their own agenda and priorities.

So the role of the professional(s) in your group is an important decision. Indicate with a check the option you consider most appropriate for your group:

_____ Professionals acting as concerned citizens, as 100% of the group

_____ Professionals as one-half the organization

_____ Professionals as a smaller fraction

_____ Membership limited to citizens plus those professionals willing to act as citizen-advocates or technical resource people

_____ Professionals called on outside of meetings as information sources or as the targets of change efforts

_____ Professionals brought into meetings by invitation only

_____ Other: _____

THE AGENCY LIAISON PERSON

One type of professional who poses a unique sort of question is the agency citizen participation liaison. If yours is the type of group which will communicate with an agency through such an intermediary, consider the following questions:

- *Is the citizen liaison person likely to be an asset to you by providing information or by advocating on your behalf within the agency?*

- *Alternately, is the liaison person likely to be a hindrance to you by proposing business which is irrelevant or by undermining the group's efforts to produce change?*

- *Will the liaison person lead the group toward more effective involvement or resist the group's efforts to develop clout?*

- *What influence can the citizens exert over the liaison person's role — at the first, and later on?*

BALANCED MEMBERSHIP

One of the hardest but perhaps the most important thing for a young organization to achieve is an appropriate balance of members — a group representative of the different interests, perspectives and communities that have a concern about the issues in question.

Instead of balanced membership, an organization will usually start out skewed in one direction or another. There are certain population groups that are more active in public affairs — especially better educated white professional males with higher incomes. Then there is the tendency for organizers to recruit their friends, neighbors and acquaintances. The organizers will probably attract people from similar ethnic, cultural, economic, educational and political background to themselves, if only because those are the people who are most confortable with the organizational style and the meeting process and content.

The following questions are designed to help you recruit a more representative and balanced group of people concerned about your issues:

- *Who's missing from your group? Turn to the list of population sub-groups in the diagnostic questionnaire on page 49 of this manual; if your group is quite new, you will be anticipating which groups will be under-represented.*

- *Which population groups are most likely to have an interest in your group's goals and issues?*

- *Which under-represented groups should get priority for recruitment?*

- *What planned goals and methods of your organization must change to make it more attractive to these people?*

- *What steps will you take to achieve balanced participation?*

Part 2:
Purposes, Structures and Methods

CHECKLIST FOR PURPOSES

Development of organizational purposes and plans is the topic of another CITP training manual, **Planning, for a Change**. This planning guide, therefore, contains only a brief checklist to help you determine whether you need to give more attention to your purposes (goals and objectives) and to your analysis of the problem you're dealing with:

a) Our citizen group has a clear diagnosis of the causes of the problems we're tackling . . .
    ( ) yes   ( ) no
    . . . written down in clear, understandable language . . .
    ( ) yes   ( ) no
    . . . and I agree with it or most of it.
    ( ) yes   ( ) no

b) Our group has a clear and forceful statement of purposes. . .
    ( ) yes   ( ) no
    . . . in terms that prospective group members can easily comprehend and relate to.
    ( ) yes   ( ) no

c) Our group has a list of current objectives — targets for the next few months or perhaps a year
    ( ) yes   ( ) no
    . . . which seem challenging but winnable
    ( ) yes   ( ) no
    . . . and which corresponds with the day-to-day activities of the group
    ( ) yes   ( ) no

If you answered no to any of these questions, what action (if any) do you believe the group should take? What could you do to initiate that action?

> **The people, I say, are the only competent judges of their own welfare.**
>
> — Josiah Quincy, 1774

WHAT TYPE OF ORGANIZATION?

Refer to the table of different forms of citizen involvement (pages 26-43). Identify the possible forms which your group could take (or the actual form, if it has been determined). Write them here. Possible forms:

#1 _____

#2 _____

#3 _____

Then answer the discussion questions on page 43. Give particular attention to this question: what can you do at this point to give your group the form or structure which will have the most influence and effectiveness?

METHODS: WHAT'S YOUR STYLE?

Even after you've chosen the **form** your organization will take, there's a question of style, of preferred methods, which is still open. Here are some possibilities; check as many as seem desirable or attractive to you.

Do you think your organization should adopt...

( ) a cooperative approach toward the agencies and organizations it relates to;

( ) or, a confrontation style;

( ) an advocacy role, speaking on behalf of one or many citizens who have been unable to get action on their problems alone;

( ) direct action as a primary tactic (examples: civil-rights sit-ins, anti-nuclear power "occupation," farmers' tractor parades, etc.);

( ) legal/court action as a primary tactic (example: Ralph Nader's consumer organizations);

( ) an advisory role;

( ) or, a role as actual decision makers, with shared or exclusive control over some aspect of policy;

( ) a reactive role, responding to injustices, inequities, and bad decisions by decision-makers;

( ) or, a "proactive" role, initiating policy ideas and programs;

( ) a thoughtful, well-reasoned approach in all positions and other written materials;

( ) a tough, "force-to-be-reckoned-with" approach in all activities and statements;

( ) a cautious approach—making sure you can win before you start anything;

( ) vs. a risk-taking approach—willing to "stick the group's neck out" for causes which may be unpopular or unwinnable;

( ) a friendly, warm style within the group, a sense of being concerned about each other as people;

( ) a "get down to business" approach—with a minimum of wasted time and a maximum of results;

( ) elected leaders who themselves do a large proportion of the work of the group;

( ) or, shared leadership, with everyone doing nearly equal shares of leadership and busy-work tasks.

There are other choices of organizational style which you may be able to identify. What's important is to be aware of these choices which often slip by without really being decided. Use the checklist above, talk about the answers, then try to summarize the group's opinions in a short statement on "what kind of group we'd like this to be." You may want to file the statement away and bring it out for periodic examination to see how you're doing and what you want to change.

And if you can't agree as a group what style you prefer, consider this as a hint that you may have basic issues to deal with, or you may even have the makings of two or more groups. Style is almost as important as purpose, issue, and structure in determining which people will be willing to come out and join up.

IMAGE: HOW OTHERS SEE YOU

Your choice of methods and organizational style will make a difference when you begin to appear in the public eye, in the mass media or in face-to-face sessions with decision-makers and fellow citizens. Here are some questions to help you explore ways to project your image effectively.

- *Do you want "high visibility" or a "low profile" at this point in your group's development? Perhaps low visibility now but more at a later date? (When?)*

- *What sort of mass media coverage will help you achieve your goals? What sorts of events or activities will help promote this coverage (press conferences, releases, rallies, teach-ins, etc.)?*

- *What do you want the public (and decision-makers) to know about your goals, analyses, and methods? What can you do to work within the constraints of the mass media (such as their need to keep their audience interested) and still put across your message in adequate detail? To what extent will you need to use media you control more directly, such as posters, handbills, public meetings, or small group discussions, to put your message across?*

- *What impression should the public have of your style? What sort of image should your organization's name bring to mind? Public advocate? Tough-minded and persistent? Rational and informative? Champion of good causes? Will your group's activities and the publicity they generate create the image you desire? If not, what can you do to change your image?*

For more information refer to the CITP manual, **Using the Media for Social Change.**

Part 3: Connections

The strength of your organization will depend a great deal on:
- your connection or relationship to your constitutents, who may be actual members or the broader public, or both;
- your relation to the decision-makers, which is one indication of your power;
- your relation with other organizations.

ACCOUNTABILITY: YOUR RELATION TO CONSTITUENTS

Many elected officials discount the ideas and positions of citizen groups on the grounds that only the elected officials are truly accountable to the public. They, after all, were elected by the majority of the voters; they run the risk of being removed from office next election day if the voters disapprove of their performance.

Most citizen groups don't have that kind of accountability. (A few neighborhood councils are actually elected bodies.) But every citizen group probably has some form of accountability, and the best response to the skeptical official may be to explain what your relation to your constituents is.

Check the relationship(s) to constituents which will typify your group.

___ Positions are taken by vote of all members

present, and represent the views of that number of citizens.

___ A small board makes policy, but is accountable to the entire membership through possible veto.

___ Positions are taken through open community meetings or petitions, and therefore reflect the views of a much larger number than the organization's members per se.

___ Other:_____

Discussion Questions:

- *How should your group be accountable to yourselves, the entire community, your funding sources, the sponsoring agency (if you're a mandated group), a specific segment of the public (such as "clients" of some social service agency), future generations yet unborn?*

- *How do you avoid having funding sources or persons with political position-power develop more than their fair share of influence within the group?*

- *If there is disagreement among groups of people to whom you are accountable, what can you do to resolve these differences?*

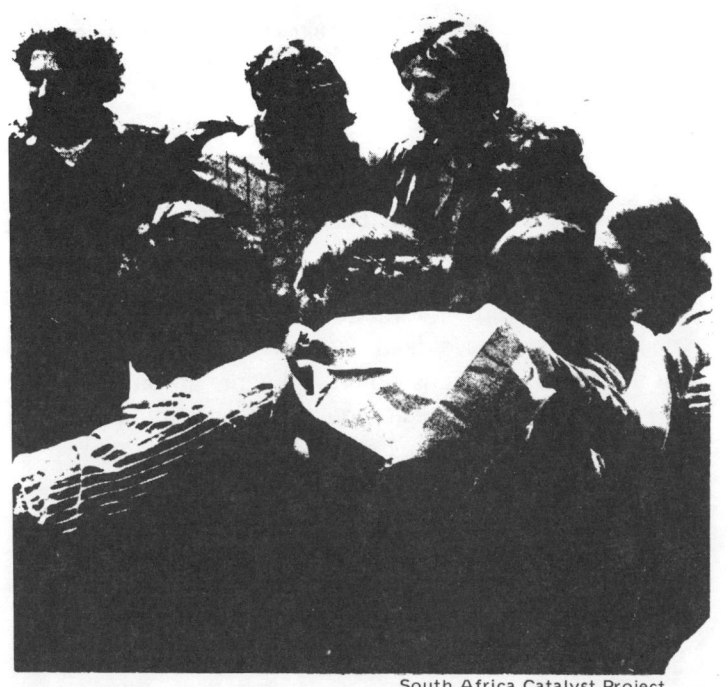

South Africa Catalyst Project

YOUR RELATION TO DECISION-MAKERS

One way to get power and to achieve your goals is to develop real influence over present decision-makers. (There are other ways to achieve power, such as by starting your own project which demonstrates better ways of doing things.) Here are some possible relations to decision-makers; put an "I" beside the one which you consider ideal; put an "L" beside the one you consider the most likely. What influence do you have over this important aspect of your organization's structure? What would you need to do first to get your ideal version?

___ No access to or influence over the relevant decision-makers

___ Recognition by decision-makers as a source of advice

___ Recognition by decision-makers as a party to decisions; shared influence

___ Recognition by decision-makers as having the power to make certain decisions; delegated power

___ Ability to influence decisions by mobilizing public opinion and bringing public pressure to bear on decision-makers (through demonstrations, educational campaigns, petition drives, citizen lobbying, etc.)

___ other:_____

YOUR RELATION TO OTHER GROUPS: TURF

Like street gangs, organizations have their "turf" staked out. A school system has a geographical area which it serves. It may also define its turf in terms of the age range it serves, the types of services it provides (subjects taught), the types of special needs which it does and does not deal with, and the sorts of things it expects other agencies to consult with it about or turn over to it.

Citizen groups, like government agencies, are prone to stake out their turf. An environmental group may get very nervous if someone tries to form a second environmental group in the same community. But things may be all right once again if it turns out that the first group is concerned with trash recycling and the second group is trying to stop industries from polluting rivers.

Make a table using the headings which follow; list the groups you expect to relate to or which share your area of concern. Make your table large enough to describe each group's turf, then pay special attention to identifying the groups with potential cooperation (indicate by a letter "C") and tension ("T").

Organization	How They Define Their Turf	C or T

Discussion Questions:

- *What can you do to minimize tension and enhance cooperation?*

- *Are there cases where you will want to promote and clarify tension, to bring differences to the public's attention?*

- *Which groups' support is especially worth going after?*

Part 4: Getting Started

There are a lot of different ways to get a new organization off the ground. Here are some common approaches; pick the one you prefer (and decide how to apply it to your situation), or develop a new one of your own.

____ Hold discussions of the issues and the need for the new organization in the homes of friends and acquaintances. Once there is enough interest, begin more formal activities.

____ Pick an issue which concerns a lot of people, one which you think you can have some influence on. Do some initial fact-finding, generate some publicity (posters, news stories), hold a public meeting, and recruit people to develop a plan of attack and get to work.

____ Start with a small group which is willing to spend months meeting as a study group, developing an analysis — an understanding of the nature of the problem — so that once you are ready to act, you will have an innovative and well-planned approach.

____ Study the needs and concerns of members or of the broader community; have these people participate in planning and developing a program which meets these needs and concerns.

____ Organize a small group of people who work quietly until an issue "breaks" — until some decision or event which signals a time when the public will want some organized way to act; then hold meetings and recruit broad-based participation.

____ Other: _____

Another CITP manual provides more information for people starting a new organization: **Power, A Repossesion Manual,** by Greg Speeter.

This Planning Guide: A Footnote

If you've answered all the questions on the preceding pages, you still have dealt with only a small fraction of the many questions which will come up on your way to a successful beginning. In this planning guide, we've focused on those issues which seem to us to have the most bearing on your chances of beginning with a significant amount of real power. We would like to know how this planning guide works for you; if you have suggestions or reactions, please send them to us at Citizen Involvement Training Project.

Improving on the Organization You've Got

We're assuming that your goal is an effective, powerful citizen group which achieves the goals and objectives which its members set for it. Most citizen groups don't do as well as they might. In this section we present some ideas for setting objectives which will make your group more effective. We then provide suggestions for strategies to implement your objectives. The activities in this section involve analyzing the barriers to effectiveness, setting goals for your group, choosing strategies, and developing detailed scenarios which will give you a "feel" for what it would be like to succeed.

Exercise:

The Transition to Citizen Power

no. people: one to many
min. time: 20 minutes
materials: form below

The form below compares aspects of the "present situation" which many groups find themselves in and an "ideal situation" which they might like to achieve. The table can be used as a discussion-starter or planning guide to help a group begin the transition toward more influence. It applies mostly to agency advisory boards and other groups which relate primarily to one agency.

Process:

1. Read through the form. Check "yes" in the column marked "Applies to Us" if you think that transition would be a useful point to focus attention for your group. At the end of the list there is space for you to add "other" items.

2. Go back to the ways in which your group is less powerful or effective than it might be. Under "TO" write the corresponding ideal ways in which your group could achieve more power.

3. Think some more about the ideal. (In a group, this can be done through brainstorming). The question to consider is: What would our group look like, and how would it operate, if it were truly effective and powerful?

4. Decide which transitions ("FROM...TO...") would be the most helpful and productive in strengthening your group. Put a priority number in the circle provided.

5. Now, the hard part: How do you get from here to there? Pick one transition step and focus your energies on ways to do it. What would need to happen? Who could help? Etc. The strategy suggestions on the following pages will aid your thinking.

FROM: Acceptance of Limitations	TO: More Power and Influence	Applies to Us	Priority	HOW
Advisory role (gentle suggestions)	Shared decision-making	___ yes ___ no		
	"Force-to-be-reckoned-with" image	___ yes ___ no		
	Sign-off power on programs and budgets	___ yes ___ no		
Accepting agency rationales ("Here's why we do things the way we do...")	Challenging procedures and assumptions	___ yes ___ no		

68

FROM: Acceptance of Limitations	TO: More Power and Influence	Applies to Us	Priority	HOW
Agency staffer sets agenda	Citizen organization as a whole sets own agendas, which are stimulating, relevant, and based on the shared personal concerns of the members	___ yes ___ no		
Reactive (responding to plans and activities of agencies and others)	Proactive (sets own goals; develops plans and strategies to achieve them)	___ yes ___ no		
Accepting agency (government) guidelines for citizen group action	Setting standards for agency or government performance	___ yes ___ no		
	Going beyond official mandate when appropriate to deal with shared concerns	___ yes ___ no		
No budgetary control	Operating budget for citizen group (technical help, travel, project funds, research, public education, outreach/publicity)	___ yes ___ no		
	Review or control over agency budget	___ yes ___ no		
Limited functions	Broader functions	___ yes ___ no		
Other				

Developing Transition Strategies: A Case Study

In the previous exercise you picked some objectives for making your group more powerful; how do you take action on them? This section is a case study — the development of one strategy which may help you to make the transition to taking more effective advantage of current legislation and regulations.

The executive branches of federal and state government are run according to the legislation which created them and the administrative regulations which add detail to the legislative guidelines. There are several types of guidelines which citizen groups can utilize to advantage.

- Citizen participation is mandated in the founding legislation and regulations of an agency or program. A summary of federal citizen participation requirements is found the the 1977 booklet, Citizen Participation, prepared by the Community Services Administration in cooperation with the Federal Government. It is available free by writing to your Congressperson.

- Citizen participation guidelines for the specific agency program you work with can be requested from the agency (state, regional, or local offices). Tracking down these guidelines and studying them carefully can be the first step toward demanding and getting all the influence to which the law entitles you. As you study the booklet on Citizen Participation or talk to agency officials, you may be referred to CFR numbers.

CFR stands for the Code of Federal Regulations, which is the print-out of all agency operating regulations. There are designated libraries across the country which carry the CFR volumes (they are referred to as "federal repository libraries"). Don't be intimidated by the legal-sounding reference (45CFR101.2, for example); the libraries will have trained reference librarians to help you track down what you're after. They may even be able to help you understand what it says, or you can make a photocopy and study it at your leisure.

- Printed matter is not the only source of information on citizen participation requirements; you can ask agency officials what the citizen participation guidelines are. If you do both, you can compare the printed guidelines with the officials' understanding, to see whether the agency knows the guidelines.

- You may start to acquire a good deal of information, and you'll need a way to organize it. One possibility is a table like this:

The printed requirements for citizen participation	What the agency says	What actually happens	Targets (*)
1.			
2.			

Title 40—Protection of Environment
Subpart D—EPA Public Hearings on Environmental Impact Statements

§ 6.100 General.
While EPA is not required by statute to hold public hearings on EIS's, the responsible official should hold a public hearing on a draft EIS whenever a hearing may facilitate the resolution of conflicts or significant public controversy. This hearing may be in addition to public hearings held on facilities plans or section 209 plans. The responsible official may take special measures to involve interested persons through personal contact.

§ 6.102 Public hearing process.
(a) When public hearings are to be held, EPA shall inform the public of the hearing, for example, with a notice in the draft EIS. The notice should follow the summary sheet at the beginning of the EIS. The draft EIS shall be available for public review at least thirty (30) days before the public hearing. Public notice shall be given at least fifteen (15) working days before the public hearing and shall include:
(1) Publication of a public notice in a newspaper which covers the project area, identifying the project, announcing the date, time and place of the hearing and announcing the availability of detailed information on the proposed action for public inspection at one or more locations in the area in which the project will be located. "De-

tailed information" shall include a copy of the project application the draft EIS.
(2) Notification of appropriate S and local agencies and approp State, regional and metrop clearinghouses.
(3) Notification of intereste sons.
(b) A written record of the shall be made. A stenographer used to record the hearing. A mum, the record shall contain witnesses with the text of eac tation. A summary of the cluding the issues raised, c solved and unresolved, and significant portions of shall be appended to the fi (c) When a public hear by another Fede ney on an EPA are not

Exercise:

Holding an Agency to Its Citizen Participation Guidelines

no. people: one to many
min. time: 30 minutes (after completing background research described above)
materials: research notes, form like one above

The purpose of this activity is to develop a plan for holding an agency accountable to its own citizen participation guidelines.

Process:

1. Gather whatever information you can about the citizen participation guidelines of the agency you work with: printed, verbal, whatever.

2. Summarize the information in a table like the one above. Make a separate number for each major point, such as:

    a. Council membership: 10 citizens representing diverse interests. . .
    (source: 40CFR20.1)

    b. Regular meetings at least once/month . . .
    (source: . . .)

3. Summarize the agency's verbal statements; for "Source" put the name of the person who provided the information.

4. Think about what happens in reality, especially regarding each point covered by regulations or the verbal statements.

5. In the right hand column, put a star beside each item where there is a significant gap between guideline and reality (or between guideline and agency understanding). These are the targeted gaps in citizen participation.

6. Now, (and you'll need at least another half hour for this — maybe several meetings), figure out which targets you want to aim for first, and develop strategies for doing something about them.

Exercise:

Developing Real Input into Policy

no. of people: five to many; one of them will have studied this workshop plan and will be prepared to "facilitate"
min. time: 2 hours
materials: newsprint, felt pens, tape

The following workshop plan was actually carried out in June of 1978; CITP worked with a citizen organization which was mandated to make input to policy planning for a planning project which was set up to develop plans for community-based care of people who are currently institutionalized. The citizen group's mandate suggested that it could and should have a strong voice in policy; the group was dissatisfied with the level of influence it had so far achieved.

The goal of the workshop was to decide how to get real citizen input into policy. The workshop plan is presented below in a general form which other groups could follow. The outcomes from the original group are in the box to the right.

Process:

1. Write the goal — "to get real citizen input into policy" — at the top of a sheet of newsprint. Ask the group to call out ways in which this goal could be implemented.

2. Your list of "Possible ways to get real citizen input" will almost certainly contain a mixture of objectives and methods for reaching those objectives. Divide a sheet of newsprint with a verticle line, and write "objectives" and "methods" at the top of the columns. Take each item from your first list and decide whether it is an objective, a method, or both; write it under the appropriate column(s). If an objective or method is missing, try to decide what it would be. Remember, there is almost always more than one method which can be used to meet a particular objective.

3. Add additional objectives or methods to the list — now, or at any point that you (the group) think of them.

4. Decide which objectives would be considered first. Which objectives are:
   - least important?
   - most important?
   - most easily accomplished?
   - most winnable?

   A straw vote could be taken.

5. Generate more methods or tactics to achieve the first priority objective. (You will already have chosen one tactic for each objective in Step 2. You will want to generate several so that you can choose the best ones and sequence them into a strategy.)

   - Choose the most promising methods ("tactics") and sequence them in an overall "strategy."

   - Summarize these decisions on a "What/How/Who/When" Worksheet (see below). Decide who will take primary responsibility for carrying out a particular tactic and who will assist. You may want to designate one person to take overall responsibility for coordinating the strategy. Set deadlines for each step.

- Go to it!

Results from June, 1978, Workshop:

Possible ways to get real citizen input into policy:

- Demand evening meetings of policy committee.
- Demand that policy committee meet at area offices throughout region.
- Advertise policy meetings to citizen groups.
- Resolve whether meetings are open to public by getting 60 people there.
- Ask for clarification on at least one point a week from policy committee.
- Raise objections (if any) to way policy committee operates (regularly).
- Set up rotating schedule of citizen representatives to policy committee meetings.
- Write the funding source saying citizen participation in policy is inadequate.

Objective	Method
Make policy group's meetings open.	Get 60 people there.
Arrange evening meetings of policy group (not just during working hours).	Demand at least one evening meeting per month.
Arrange meetings at area offices (not just at regional office).	Demand rotating schedule of locations.
Let people know where/when policy meetings are, and whether or not they are open.	Advertise and publicize.
Citizen group representation on policy group.	Establish rotation schedule of citizen group representatives to share this work.
Let them know we're watching.	Ask for clarification on one point a week (at least).
Review policies.	Make substantive objections and constructive criticism.
Make policy inputs **before** decisions.	Raise objections about procedure.
Challenge adequacy of citizen participation activities.	Write a letter to Washington.

Additional Objectives:

Re-establish prestige of the citizen committee. Identify problems which the policy committee should address. Train people to carry on the citizen participation after this specific planning project is over.

Priority Objectives:

(The method actually used to identify the most important objectives was for each person to state preferences, followed by a straw vote.)

1. Get more membership on the citizen committee.
2. Get citizen group members more involved.
3. Have the citizen committee make policy inputs **before** the policy committee makes decisions.

Possible Tactics (Methods) for Achieving the Primary Objectives:

- Canvass the local citizen groups.

- Get knowledge of need.

- Obtain packet of needs survey fingings from area planners.

- Ask for information from the regional work group.

- Find out what they are about to make policy on.

- Define your own value base first.

- Ask the policy group to make specific policies.

- Let them (policy group) know you're watching.

- Understand the policy review process and its timing.

- Slow down the process (ask the policy group for more time, if needed, for citizen group to generate/review policy. Get more time between the initial policy proposal and formal discussion of it).

- Make your own policy as a citizen group.

- Publicize issues in wider community.

- Ask other citizens to get involved.

- Quit your job and be a (citizen involved in policy) 24 hours a day.

(Notice that some tactics appeared on the earlier list of objectives. In building strategies, one always identifies targets which become stepping stones to broader objectives.)

Sample Form

WHAT	HOW	WHO	WHEN			
Object/Project--What has to be done.	Methods/Procedures/Tactics	Whose responsibility--The whole group, a committee, an individual. (Names)	Timetable			
			August	September	October	
1) Get more evening meetings.	1) Request evening meetings.		xxx			
	2) If necessary, call director of agency.			xx		
	3) If necessary, call Washington.			xxxx		
2) Get policy committee to meet at area offices.	1) etc.					
3)						

75

WHAT	HOW	WHO	WHEN
Object/Project--What has to be done.	Methods/Procedures/Tactics	Whose responsibility--The whole group, a committee, an individual. (Names)	Timetable
1)			
2)			
3)			

80 Ways to Enhance Your Group's Clout

This manual has featured only some of the ways to make your citizen group more effective. Here is a "laundry list" of ideas—a review of those in the manual, plus a good number of others which may turn out to be more appropriate for your situation. Only you and your group can decide what steps you need to take.

It's a matter of having enough hands and minds to get the job done, and a broad enough base of support to win the respect of decision—makers.

Membership

1. Get more members.
2. Get more diversity of membership.
3. Get members more involved: put everyone in charge of something.
4. Determine whether membership represents an appropriate cross-section of the community.
5. Involve families in your projects.
6. Try to build a solid consensus of support for activities, when someone consistently wants to go off in a different direction, ask him either to stop blocking consensus or to leave.
7. Provide ways for people who aren't active members to show support, such as petitions, associate memberships or financial contributions.

Analysis

8. Develop an independent understanding of the causes of social problems.
9. Identify and challenge the assumptions about problems made by decision-makers.
10. For a part of every meeting discuss analyses of social problems and their political and economic roots.
11. Understand national trends, especially those which concern many people; build support for your program by showing its relationship to major trends.
12. Understand their concerns, viewpoints and priorities of your enemies and allies.
13. Define your ideal; envision a society in which your group's issue, and other problems which concern you, have been resolved.

If problems persist, it is probably because established solutions don't address the root causes.

Structure

14. Research government requirements for citizen involvement in the issue-area which concerns you.

The question of structure is the question of your group's relation to power—your ability to see your decisions put into effect.

Fulfilling the letter of the law regarding citizen participation may not be enough; you want them to fulfill the **spirit** of citizen participation requirements.

If you can't go **through**, go **around**.

If you can't get control over the agency budget, develop your own budget analysis and a "counter-budget." Show how you counter-budget would be better.

Restaurants advertise "new management" to project a more exciting image. Citizen groups could issue press releases about their "new management," projecting a tougher more powerful image.

15. Identify ways in which requirements for participation are not being fulfilled.
16. Present a list of inadequacies to the agency, with recommended improvements.
17. Publicize inadequacies and desired changes through the mass media.
18. Take legal action to hold agency to citizen participation requirements.
19. Identify ways in which **requirements** are inadequate.
20. Lobby for more stringent requirements for citizen participation.
21. Confront agency attitude toward citizen participation.
22. Press for dismissal or reassignment of agency citizen involvement personnel who are unresponsive to citizen views or unwilling to advocate for citizen views within their agency.
23. Go directly to decision-makers; by-pass anyone who seems to act only as a buffer between agency and citizens.
24. Go to the top if you need to. Also, don't overlook the possibility that the direct service worker—the highway engineer, the social worker, the school teacher—may be more accessible and more willing to change than "the boss" is.
25. Take a mayor to lunch.
26. Assign one citizen group member to each relevant decision-maker—to lobby, to research (voting record, interest, etc.)
27. Develop new ways of solving a problem which by-pass uncooperative decision-makers.
28. Acquire direct control over some decisions (through legislative lobbying or agency delegation of power).
29. Acquire shared control over some decisions.
30. Especially, acquire some degree of control over budget—not just a "sign-off" (veto power), but a say in what does and doesn't go in.
31. Become more independent from any agency you wish to influence. For instance, if you depend on that agency for funds for you citizen group operations, acquire an independent source of funds.
32. Brainstorm other structural alternatives which would give your group more power; decide which ones to implement and then implement them.

Image; "Posture"

33. Develop a more forceful image—tougher language, a clear impression that you'll stick to it until you get what you're after. In general, a more vigorous stance or "posture."
34. Elect new leaders willing to adopt a more forceful image.
35. Change the name of your group; choose a "tougher" name.
36. Consider not using the phrase "citizen participation," which is sometimes connected with polite, advisory forms of input with little influence.
37. Become better known (a "household word").
38. Launch a public education campaign.
39. Get radio and TV stations to help you develop your own

public service announcements for broadcast.
40. Go on local cable television.
41. Get listed or featured in other groups' newsletters.
42. Start or improve your own newsletter and send it to as many influential people as possible.
43. Leaders and other members should adopt the attitude that "we are a high profile group"—the public **needs** to know about us, our thinking and our positions on issues.
44. Raise the consciousness of the general public: what it means to be an active, effective citizen.

Strategies and Forms of Involvement

See the table of Forms of Citizen Participation in Part I of this manual.

45. Understand the form of citizen participation which your group reptresents.
46. Decide whether your group would be more effective by taking a different form of involvement or using a different strategy. If so, figure out how to change and do so.
47. Demand to be heard at the times you want, not just the times the decision-makers invite you to speak.
48. Set up a demonstration or "alternative" project. Decide how a problem should really be dealt with, get funding if you really need it, and show 'em how it ought to be done.
49. Canvass neighborhoods to gather opinions and build support.
50. Support community issues and concerns.
51. Celebrate community events (holidays, local history, successes).
52. Hold block parties.
53. Get police and other local officials on your side.
54. Choose winnable issues.
55. Hire a lawyer and an ad agency.
56. Threaten to take legal action.
57. Take legal action on your issue.

Citizen Involvement as an Issue

58. Announce a campaign for better citizen involvement.
59. List past citizen requests and recommendations; distinguish those which decision-makers did and didn't respond to.
60. Identify types of input which may not be responded to in the future.
61. Issue a white paper of findings from previous three steps.
62. Plan to negotiate with decision-makers on those decisions which have consistently not been responded to, plan to use strategies which put additional pressure on decision-makers or plan to by-pass them.
63. Get the support of other citizen groups who also feel they haven't been given a fair shake.

Another CITP manual, **Planning, for a Change,** will provide a procedure for "force-field analysis" and help you clarify goals.

64. Analyze the forces which are limiting your power, holding you back from your goal of an appropriate, significant level of influence.
65. Clarify your goals for improving your citizen participation mechanism—your access to power, to information, etc.

"We are not listening to your demands until you agree to accept what we offer."

PHS. New Unity

> Any real change in the status quo depends on continued creative action to sharpen the conscience of the nation and establish a climate in which even the most recalcitrant elements are forced to admit that change is necessary.
> — Martin Luther King

66. **Assume** that you have the power you would like—start acting as if you have it.
67. Set up a shadow government or shadow agency—a citizen committee which would make all the decisions which officials are making, presumably with different outcomes. Analyze the impacts of their decisions and yours, and issue a report comparing the desirability of the two different sets of policies.

Resources and Assistance

68. Acquire a budget for your citizen involvement activities, preferably from a source which will not want to sway your decisions regarding policies and activities.
69. Assess organizational history and strengths; they are among your most important resources.
70. Use community resources such as school building for space.
71. Draw on technical experts for advice and testimony.
72. Enlist the support of people with clout.
73. Use process consultants and facilitators when appropriate.
74. Seek in-kind services (free printing, auditing, legal assistance, etc.).

Organizational Development

75. Take charge of your own agenda; determine your own priorities and long-range goals; allocate time in accordance with them.
76. Develop a stance of initiating plans and policies rather than reacting to those of some government agency or other organization.
77. Manage time carefully and realistically, both within a single meeting and over months and years as you attempt to implement your plans.
78. Develop leadership and membership skills. Make training an on-going part of your activities.
79. Run your organization in ways which anticipate the sort of world you are trying to create. For example, you may want to minimize top-down decision-making and emphasize consensus decision making. You should attempt to avoid the prejudicial behaviors common in society at large regarding class, race, sex and age.
80. Evaluate your progress regularly and take whatever steps are necessary to keep events headed toward the goals you seek.

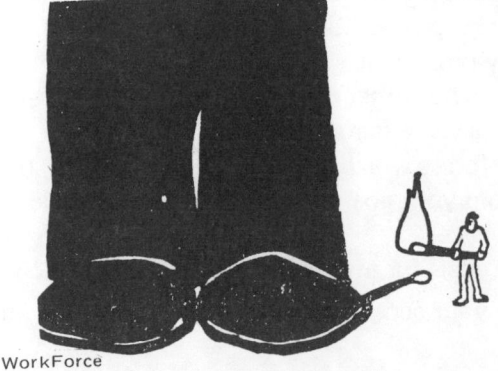

WorkForce

Notes to the Individual Citizen

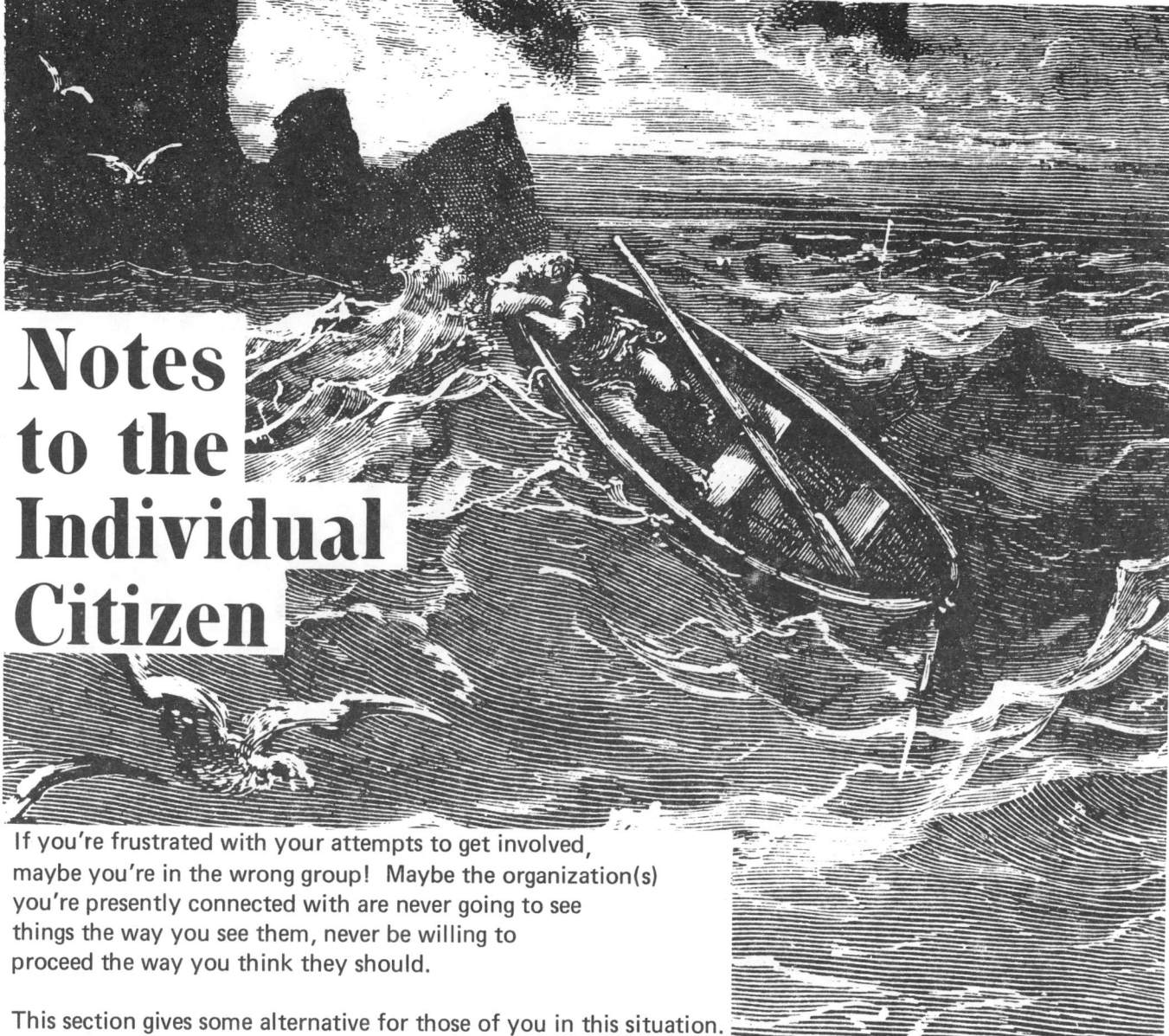

If you're frustrated with your attempts to get involved, maybe you're in the wrong group! Maybe the organization(s) you're presently connected with are never going to see things the way you see them, never be willing to proceed the way you think they should.

This section gives some alternative for those of you in this situation.

Or maybe you're not involved in any citizen group right now—because you got turned off or because you never got started. There are suggestions for you as well.

The section includes four considerations:

- Choosing your issue— one that really motivates you.
- Choosing organizational styles and strategies— spotting the groups that share your assumptions about the ways to act to achieve power and effectiveness.
- Surveying the options—what groups are out there, how effective they are and how happy you'd be working with them.
- Starting something yourself—a new group, committee, board, task force, research group, council, party or movement.

Choosing Your Issue

You're not going to get very far fighting someone else's battles. Probably the best prescription for keeping your energy high for citizen involvement is to know your issue, to know exactly why you want to be involved. For example, even if your main concern is better housing, you might not be excited by a group that is promoting housing rehabilitation. You could go looking for a group (or individuals) who want to try a different approach—such as enforcing housing codes. Before you do that, it might make sense to consider some basic questions.

- What really concerns you as an individual and as a member of society?
- What are some of the ways your life and the lives of others could be better, some of the problems that really get to you, things that bug you on a day-to-day basis?
- How are these concerns of yours similar to groups that you know of? How are they different?

Suggestion: Don't just read through these quickly—sit down with a neighbor, friend or family member and ask them to listen as you think through these things out loud. Or get your group to designate time for these questions. People should choose a partner and spend perhaps ten to fifteen minutes each, giving their answers while the other person listens. The benefit for the group is like the benefit for an individual: people can get in touch with the sources of their own motivation and energy.

Questions to Ask Before Joining a Citizen Board

- *Who has the organizational authority for the participation process?*

- *Who defines the responsibilities of the participating citizens?*

- *What are the procedures for the selection of citizens?*

- *Is there staff and budget support for the process of selecting citizens to participate and for their efforts when selected?*

- *Does the staff get in the way of citizens, keeping citizens from making key decisions?*

- *Is there a procedure to review or investigate complaints about the selection of citizens and the operation of committees, councils, etc., including the process for response after a review is completed?*

- *What is the means by which information is made available to participants?*

- *What is the role of citizens in the development of a citizen participation plan or process?*

- *Is participation really going to make a difference?*

Does the Citizen Participation Plan Include . . .

- a statement of the project goals and the goals of participation?

- a statement delineating responsibilities, including the relationship of the program to the organization and the roles of participating citizens, state and the department or unit to which it relates?

- identify constraints (time, budget, etc.) to be considered?

- a statement identifying provisions of needed state and federal codes, including ways citizens can file complaints and requests for review?

- a statement of the procedures to be followed for establishing dates of meetings, hearings, etc., how they get on the master calendar, and who disseminates the information, etc?

- a definition of procedures for reports and recommendations and a list of when and who should receive them?

- a plan for the dissemination of information?

Does the Agency Have . . .

- an open door policy which allows citizens to talk to officials?

- office meetings of officials with individuals or small groups to discuss public policy programs, etc.

- meetings with community organizations? Does it exclude certain organizations? Which ones? Why?

- use of citizen committees, advisory and other planning councils?

- public hearings?

- informal briefings and a discussion of priorities, goals, programs, budget, etc?

- bilingual services when appropriate?

How Well Does the Agency Provide Information?

- Does it provide timely and accurate answers to questions?

- Does it provide announcements of plans, programs, hearings, etc., through news and public service programs of the media (bilingually when appropriate)?

- Have copies or summaries of reports, proposed legislation and other materials been made available (bilingually when appropriate) for the interested?

- Have outlines of public procedures been made available for distribution to the public on planning, budget, legislative procedures, etc., including identification of key stages and time tables and how and when to maximize input?

- Have background materials been made accessible to you?

- Have you been given the evaluation standards and procedures for each program?

- Have you been given adequate background material for public hearings together with clear information on the steps to take when testifying at a hearing or filing written testimony?

- Have periodic programs and legislative briefings been made available for community leaders and the staffs of consumer-oriented organizations?

Voting With Your Feet

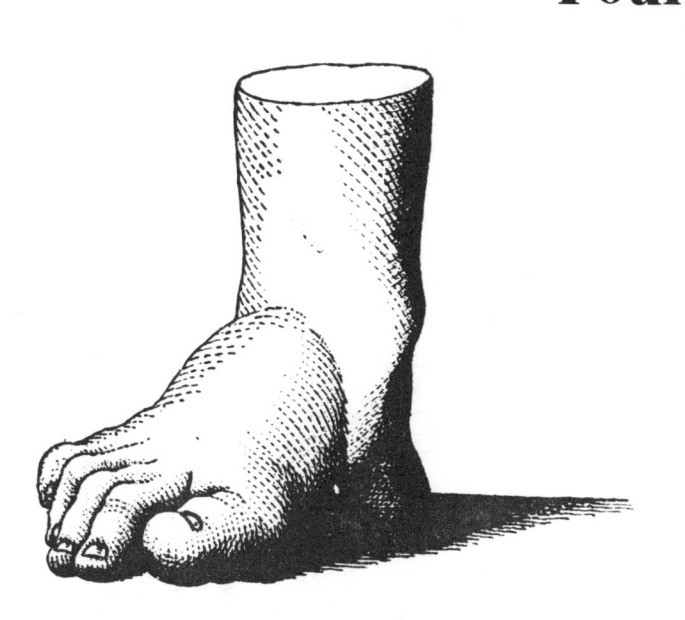

When and How to Quit

There are times when it seems as if involvement in a citizen group isn't leading anywhere. The meetings are boring, and there's no progress to show for them.

If you are a member of a citizen group who's frustrated and considering resignation, we have two bits of advice.

1) Think very carefully about whether you're the person who can help the group find its full power and effectiveness. We hope the ideas in this manual will help you. Let other members know you're dissatisfied and why. Dare to violate the norm most groups have which says "we're doing fine, and anyone who doubts it is a trouble-maker."

2) If there's still no way out, no match between you and the group, no chance for effectiveness as things stand now, don't quit quietly—go out with a bang. A letter to the group, or perhaps to a newspaper, if responsibly done, may jar the group into taking a new outlook. It should explain your reasons for leaving and, if possible, reiterate the actions or changes which you have been urging the group to undertake.

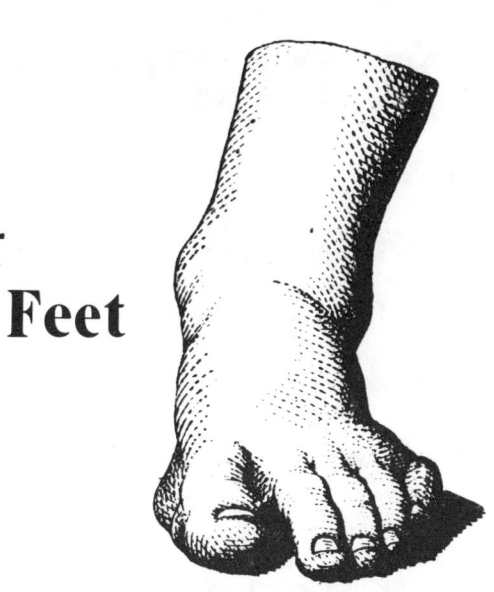

Sticking With It

Whether you stay or leave, the most important perspective to gain is that producing meaningful social change through citizen involvement is a long-term process. None of the ideas in this manual for restructuring your citizen group can be done overnight. Some will take years before the changes in effectiveness begin to show. Moreover, the issues that groups fight for — a clean environment, better housing, education and jobs, access to health care, and so on — these problems are so much a part of the status quo that change will come slowly in most cases.

But changes can occur, and they have occurred in many areas. At the start of the environmental movement, many corporate executives were inclined to "wait it out" — to give this latest fad in citizen movements time to pass away before they invested heavily in air- or water-cleaning devices, emission control systems, etc. Rather than pass away, the environmental movement went to the legislatures and the courts. Although far from a total success, it has produced such victories as a marked increase in the number of swimmable rivers in this country.

Other issues are harder. (Corporate executives like the rest of us have a stake in a clean environment.) When economic injustice is confronted in this country or around the world, there are people who benefit from the oppression of others. This makes hunger, landlessness and poverty very hard to deal with.

None of these problems will change if the good people of the world stand by and say nothing. But, we believe, no force can prevent change if the people of the world stand up and demand it.

RESOURCES

For convenient reference, materials and organizations are listed in the following groupings:

1. References (works cited in this manual)

2. Anthologies and Other General Works on Citizen Participation

3. Government Agency Studies and Reports on Citizen Participation

4. Comparative Listings of Citizen Participation Forms

5. Citizen Action Guides

6. Techniques and Skills for Citizen Groups

7. Demonstration Projects: Local-Level Citizen Involvement

8. Future-Oriented Citizen Involvement

9. Community Research

10. Resource Organizations

11. Other Bibliographies

1. References (Works Cited in This Manual)

Constructive Citizen Participation
Quarterly Newsletter
Development Press
Box 1016
Oakville, Ontario, CANADA
$4.00/year for students and volunteer leaders; $12.00/year for organizations.

The Crisis of Democracy: Report on the Governability of Democracies to the Trilateral Commission
Michael Crozier, Samuel P. Huntington and Joji Watanuki
New York University Press, 1975
$4.95

Education for Critical Consciousness
Paulo Freire
Seabury Press, 1973
$2.95

Freire's insightful analysis and method for adult education which can heighten citizen awareness and provide the basis for involvement and action.

"A Ladder of Citizen Participation"
Sherry Arnstein
Journal of the American Institute of Planners, Vol. 35 (July, 1969), pp. 216-224.

The Power Broker: Robert Moses and the Fall of New York
Robert A. Caro
Alfred A. Knopf, 1974

"Is This Any Way to Start a Revolution?"
Edward Schwartz
Social Policy, (July - August 1974), pp. 10-11.

Published by Social Policy Corporation, New York, New York 10036
Reprinted by Permission

Poor People's Movements: Why They Succeed, How They Fail
Frances Fox Piven and Richard Cloward
Pantheon Books, 1977.

Analyzes four social movements of the 20th Century: the unemployed workers' movement, the industrial workers' movement, the Civil Rights Movement, and the Welfare Rights Movement. Thought-provoking analysis and recommendations for future actions.

Report of the Massachusetts Governor's Commission on Citizen Participation, 1973

State Documents Office
State House
Boston, Mass. 02133

Social Inventions
Stuart D. Conger
Saskatchewan Newstart, 1974

A catalog of social institutions, giving a brief description and the date and place they were "invented."

The Structure of Urban Reform
Roland Warren, Stephen Rose and Ann Burgunder
Lexington Books, 1974

TVA and the Grassroots
Philip Selznick
Harper Torchbook, 1966

2. Anthologies and Other General Works on Citizen Participation

Citizen Participation: A Case Book in Democracy
edited by Edgar S. Cahn and Barry A. Passett
New Jersey Community Action Training Institute, 1970
2465 S. Broad St.
Trenton, New Jersey

A fine anthology with varied case studies and an overview of citizen participation in the 1960s.

Citizen Participation Certification for Community Development: A Reader on the Citizen Participation Process
Patricia Marshall, editor
National Association of Housing and Redevelopment Officials, 1977
2600 Virginia Avenue, N.W.
Washington, D.C. 20037
$9.50.

A good primer on citizen involvement in community planning. The section on techniques and processes for citizen participation includes: organizing for citizen participation, public hearings, committees and sub committees, selecting a representative group, the committee process, starting the citizen participation process, organizational partnership, working with the media, citizen surveys, small group techniques, advocacy, 20th century town meetings, etc.

Citizen Participation in America
Stuart Langton
Lexington Books, 1978

No republic ever yet stood on a stable foundation without satisfying the common people.
— Mercy Warren, 1788

Nine essays covering the state of the art in citizen participation practices, grass-roots and federal perspectives, a review of research, an analysis in light of democratic theory, and a guide to planning citizen participation activities. The book was written for initial distribution at the 1978 National Conference on Citizen Participation in Washington, D.C.

3. Government Agency Studies and Reports on Citizen Participation

The recent pressure for more citizen voice in federal policy-making and program administration have inspired quite a number of new requirements as well as reports and studies. Here are a few examples:

Citizen Organizations: Increasing Client Control Over Services
Robert Yin, William A. Lucas, Peter L. Szanton and J. Andrew J. Andrew Spindler
Prepared for the Dept. of Health, Education and Welfare by the RAND Corporation

Useful summaries of research and theory regarding participation in social service programs and planning.

Citizen Participation
Community Services Administration, 1978
Available free through your Congressperson

A directory of federal programs which have citizen participation components and requirements, including a brief summary of the requirements and cross reference numbers to the mandating legislation and regulations.

At Square One: Proceedings of the Conference on Citizen Participation in Government Decision Making

Federal Interagency Council on Citizen Participation, 1977
A limited supply is available by writing
Mr. Ron Hoffman, Executive Secretariat
Office of the Secretary,
Department of the Interior
18th and E Streets, N.W.
Washington, D.C. 20240
Free

The heart of the report "Government Constraints in Working with the Public" and "Public Constraints in Working with the Government" are divided into several problem statements, each with discussion, possible remedies, and an indicator statement section. Articles include: "A Case for Citizen Participation," "Limitations and Constraints on Effective Citizen Particiaption," and a panel discussion on "The Outlook for Citizen Participation." Very readable.

Several additional federal agency reports are included in the next section.

---

4. Comparative Listings of Citizen Participation Forms

These materials were important resources in the preparation of the section of this manual titled "The Forms of Citizen Participation."

"Citizen Participation for Urban Management"
Jonathan L. Benson, Richard C. Conway and Thomas E. James, Jr.
Mershon Center Quarterly Report 3(2), Winter, 1978, pp.4-5.

Community Involvement in Highway Planning: A Manual of Techniques
U.S. Department of Transportation, January, 1977, 360 pp. Available from the U.S. Department of Transportation, Federal Highway Administration, Office of Environmental Policy, 400 7th Street, S.W., Washington, D.C., 20590. Free.
Written for Department of Transportation personnel for use in encouraging and promoting citizen participation in the transportation planning process, this book would serve any citizen group well. There are sections on communications skills, facilitating group process and discussions, and the recorder's role at meetings. Another section concerns methods for researching the community goals and objectives, values, and priorties, local government, economic profile, social profile, non-governmental influences, and community action climate.
The heart of the book is a complete description of over 80 community involvement techniques, including objectives, procedures, costs, advantages and disadvantages.

Citizen Participation: What Others Say... What Others Do....
John Warden
Mid-Atlantic Center for Community Education
School of Education
University of Virginia
Charlottesville, Virginia 22903
1977, $1.00.

A comparison of a dozen major forms of citizen participation with references for further study.

87

5. Citizen Action Guides

Citizens, Participate! An Action Guide for Public Issues
Desmond M. Connor
Published by Development Press
Box 1016
Oakville, Ontario, Canada
1974, 63 pp.
$2.00 + Post pd.

Reviews how citizen leaders and agency staff can foster constructive public participation in planning projects. Contains sections on starting-up, collecting information, mutual education, and informing officials of public preferences. A case study and sample materials are also included.

How to Get Things Changed: A Handbook for Tackling Community Problems
Bert Strauss and Mary E. Stowe
Doubleday & Co., 1974, $8.95

Presents a case for a multi-issue federation of community activists to coordinate activities and plan strategies for dealing with persistent problems. Examples from the authors' experience in Virginia and metropolitan Washington, D.C.

The Organization and Operation of Neighborhood Councils: A Practical Guide
by Howard W. Hallman, with chapters by Hans B.C. Speigel, George J. Washnis, and Conrad Weiler, 1977, 158 pp.

Published by Praeger Publications (in cooperation with the Center for Governmental Studies),
200 Park Avenue
New York, NY, 10017
$3.95

This book reviews a variety of types of neighborhood councils, illustrated by a number of case studies, and considers such issues as their legal basis and extent of authority, initiators and opponents, technical assistance and finances, communications, relations to local government, neighborhood-operated services, and evaluation of program results. Most examples are drawn from neighborhood councils which develop in close cooperation with local governments.

Power: A Repossession Manual
Issues & Strategies for Community Organizing
Greg Speeter
Citizen Involvement Training Project, 1978
University of Massachusetts
Amherst, MA 01003

A guide to the development of powerful and effective citizen organizations, the manual goes through the basic steps of organizing, compares different approaches, and presents success models and typical problems. Special emphasis is placed on encouraging the reader to develop his/her own theory of power and social change, and to explore methods of dealing with root causes of social problems.

A Public Citizens Action Manual
Donald K. Ross
Published by Grossman Publishers, Inc.
625 Madison Avenue
New York, NY, 10022
1973, 238 pp.
$1.95

This is a "how-to" action manual that provides information, ideas, models and strategies to deal with many current problems. Of particular interest are sections on how to form a citizens lobby and how to convene and hold citizens hearings.

Working on the System: A Comprehensive Manual for Citizen Access to Federal Agencies
James R. Michael, editor
Basic Books, 1974

"Here is the distillation of Ralph Nader's years of experience in petitioning, protesting, and suing federal regulatory agencies to force them to act in the public interest...." — flyleaf

"Critical Incidents in Citizen Participation"
(videotape, 21 min., U-matic cassette, color)
Citizen Participation Training Project, 1978
Rental, $15 from Ed Sheridan
Division of Community Services
University of Washington
Seattle, Washington 98195

Fifteen short vignettes of typical problem situations in citizen participation, designed as discussion-starters for agency staff training sessions, but useful to citizen groups interested in exploring basic issues in citizen participation.

Effective Citizen Participation in Transportation Planning, Volumes 1 and 2
by U.S. Department of Transportation, 1976, Volume 1, 129 pp., Volume 2, 298 pp.
Available from the U.S. Department of Transportation, Federal Highway Administration, Economic Studies Division, 400 7th Street, S.W., Washington, DC, 20590. Free.

Volume 1—The first half of this book outlines the basic steps (19 in all) in the transportation planning process, and identifies and provides a brief description of 37 major techniques for citizen participation relating them to the most appropriate steps in this planning process outline. The second half of this book reviews eight case studies which illustrate a single technique or combination of techniques as used in various planning projects. Planning projects cited include, areas other than transportation, such as, the construction of a dam, development of a commercial section in a large metropolitan area, and the development of a regional housing policy.

Volume 2—The detailed inventory of 37 major techniques for citizen participation which can be used in a wide diversity of public planning programs. Among others, techniques include: advocacy planning, citizen training, neighborhood meetings, public information programs, workshops, citizen surveys, community technical assistance. The techniques are listed and described by way of general description and strategy, positive features, negative features, potential for resolving controversial issues, utilization in various public planning programs, costs involved, and selected bibliography for those interested in more information. A good handbook for citizen groups.

"The Future of Citizen Involvement"
Alden Lind
The Futurist (December, 1975) pp. 316-328.

> There is a growing feeling of powerlessness in America, a feeling that large public and private institutions which influence our daily lives cannot in turn be influenced by the individual citizen.... We hear our elected officials speaking to us on radio and television, but we can't effectively speak to them...
>
> — Walter Mondale
> *The Accountabilty of Power*, 1975

6. Techniques and Skills for Citizen Groups

Meetings That Get Results
Donald R. Fessler
Community Leader Training Associates, Inc.
511 Monte Vista Drive, S.W.
Blacksburg, VA 24060
1971, 17 pp.
$2.00

A clear guide which includes: factors to consider when planning a meeting, various methods of achieving audience involvement (speaker and open discussion, forum, panel discussion, open discussion, etc.), how to facilitate a discussion, brainstorming, and role playing.

Planning, for a Change
Duane Dale and Nancy Mitiguy
Citizen Involvement Training Project, 1978
University of Massachusetts
Amherst, Mass. 01003

A step-by-step guide to planning processes that individual citizens or organizations working together can utilize to develop programs. Also, suggestions on evaluation and sections on specific techniques such as force-field analysis, problem redefinition, opportunity analysis, time-lining, etc.

Resource Manual for a Living Revolution
Virginia Coover, Ellen Deacon, Charles Esser, Christopher Moore
New Society Press, 1977
Movement for a New Society
4722 Baltimore Avenue
Philadelphia, PA 19143
$4.00

Over 300 pages of theories, strategies and workshop ideas are listed in this manual, put out by members of Movement for a New Society. Sections include: the theoretical basis for change, working in groups, developing communities of support, personal growth— consciousness raising, training and education, organizing for change, exercises, and other tools.

Techniques for Organizational Effectiveness
American Association of University Women
2401 Virginia Avenue, N.W.
Washington, DC, 20037
$1.95
All orders must be prepaid.

A manual designed to assist in building a cohesive group and increasing group decision-making skills in community projects. It correlates these areas with useful "how-to" techniques to create learning situations for improving group process.

Tool Catalog — Techniques and Strategies for Successful Action Programs
American Association of University Women
2401 Virginia Avenue, N.W.
Washington, DC, 20037
$6.50 ($4.50 AAUW members)
All orders must be prepaid.

A catalog of approaches and techniques useful in planning and executing projects. Provides step-by-step processes for carrying out various techniques using low budgets and volunteers including: dealing with institutions, fact finding, publicity information techniques, organization and planning, and demonstrations of support or opposition.

The Universal Traveler
Don Koberg and Jim Bagnall
William Kaufman, Inc., 1976
$5.45

An imaginative and involving guide to creative thinking and planning processes, suitable for individual or group use. Helpful to citizen groups working at program development, problem solving, self-evaluation, societal analysis, or just needing a fresh perspective on what they're doing.

Up with the Ranks: How Community Organizers Develop Community Leadership
Mark Lindberg
NETCCO, 1977
19 Davis St.
Providence, R.I.

A handy, common-sense, easy-to-read and understand manual, describing a process of building grassroots leadership in a community.

Values Clarification: A Handbook of Practical Strategies for Teachers and Students
Sidney B. Simon, Leland W. Howe and Howard Kirschenbaum
Hart Publishing Co., 1972, $3.95

Of practical use to community group members as well as students, the book suggests ways to explore the values and preferences of members as a basis for goal-setting and program development; it also provides ways to analyze and interpret the group's recent history. Clear, straightforward directions for 79 different values-clarifying strategies.

7. Demonstration Projects: Local-Level Citizen Involvement

Community Information Expositions: Issue-Oriented Displays and Popular Understanding of Social Problems
American Association for the Advancement of Science, 1973
1515 Massachusetts Avenue, N.W.
Washington, D.C. 20005

A report on the community issue exposition at the 1972 AAAS conference in Washington, D.C. Provides thorough documentation of this particular exposition plus discussion of the merits of the format as a way to promote interest in and understanding of community issues. Lengthy bibliography.

Community Problem-Solving: The Delinquency Example
Irving A. Spergel
University of Chicago Press, 1974, $3.95

A theoretical and practical overview of strategies and steps for organizing and carrying out community action projects. Presents the delinquency case study in a way that strategies can be generalized easily to other issues.

People Power: An Alternative to 1984
Morgan J. Doughton
MediaAmerica, 1976
Bethlehem, PA.

Gives many examples of how people overcome bureaucraoratic structures and solve community problems without outside help.

Uplift: What People Themselves Can Do
Susan Davis
Olympus Publishing Co., 1974

One hundred case studies of successful self-help projects—farm cooperatives, health clinics, job-training programs, drug and alcohol rehabilitation centers, housing programs, new businesses with grass-roots origins, multi-purpose community organizations. Varied and representative selection; readable format.

8. Future-Oriented Citizen Involvement

The California Tomorrow Plan
Alfred Heller, editor
William Kauffmann, Inc., 1972

The report of a special study by citizens of California analyzing the present problems of the state and exploring two alternative scenarios for the future: "California One," with a continuation of present trends and policies, and "California Two," the result of a new set of basic policies promoting favorable trends in land use, housing, pollution control, citizen participation, etc.

89

Citizen Futures Organizations: Group Profiles

Keith Alan Bea and Cynthia Elma Huston
Published by Congressional Research Service
Available only through your congressperson
Free.

Lists and describes 29 state regional, and local organizations which develop goals for the future of their communities and encourage the participation of citizens in the setting of these goals. Brief sections on history, funding, organizational structure, method of approach, problems and accomplishments, and contact person for each group.

How to Save Urban America

William A. Caldwell, Editor
New American Library, 1973

An exploration of problems and possibilities in the greater New York area. The book was written as a supplement to newspaper articles and broadcast specials as part of the New York Regional Plan Association's "Choices for '76" campaign which culminated in a citizen ballot on major policy issues. The questions are included in this book.

"What Is Anticipatory Democarcy?"

Alvin Toffler
The Futurist, October, 1975
pp. 224-229.

Rationale and case examples for citizen involvement in long-range societal planning.

9. Community Research

Action-Research: A New Style of Politics in Education

Parker Palmer
Institute for Responsive Education
775 Commonwealth Avenue
Boston, MA 02215

Presents eight techniques for citizen fact-finding, including participation-observation.

Collecting Evidence: A Layman's Guide to Participant Observation

Joseph Ferreira and Bill Burges
Institute for Responsive Education
704 Commonwealth Avenue
Boston, MA 02215

Facts for a Change: Citizen Action Research for Better Schools

Bill Burges
Published by Institute for Responsive Education
704 Commonwealth Avenue
Boston, MA, 02215
$5.00

This manual is a citizen-action research tool, applicable and very useful for a wide range of community-defined issues. It is geared to help people think clearly about an issue and find the resources they need to face it. Included are "how-to" sections on research in analyzing techniques.

Finding Community: A Guide to Community Research and Action

W. Ron Jones
James E. Freel and Associates
Palo Alto California
1971

This book is divided into 11 chapters, each dealing with a specific problem faced by most communities (food costs, welfare, health, housing, etc.). Each chapter presents "indictments" (problem statements), brief readings, methods for community research and action, success models and positive alternatives.

How to Research your Local Bank

William Batko
Available from Institute for Local Self Reliance
1717 18th St. N.W.
Washington, DC 20009
$2.00 plus postage

A beginner's guide to researching banks. Tells where basic information is located, how to get it, and what to do with it. It also explains common banking terminology and some sample reports.

Measuring the Effectiveness of Basic Municipal Services: Initial Report

Harry P. Hatry, et.al.
Available from the Urban Institute
2100 M. Street, N.W.
Washington, DC, 20037
$4.00, prepaid.

Provides an overview of the system of procedures for monitoring and obtaining community feedback on the quality of basic municipal services. Effectiveness indicators provided from monitoring solid waste collection and disposal; recreation opportunities; library services; police protection - crime control; fire protection; local transportation; water supply, waste water treatment and water pollution; and handling of citizen complaints and requests for services. Most of the procedures for monitoring should be within the capabilities of citizen groups without elaborate equipment or extensive technical assistance.

(How Effective Are Your Community Services: Procedures for Monitoring the Effectiveness of Municipal Services is a forthcoming Urban Institute Publication which serves to complement this report by providing more detailed discussion of the data collection procedures.)

Obtaining Citizen Feedback: The Application of Citizen Surveys to Local Governments

Kenneth Webb and Harry P. Hatry
Available from The Urban Institute
2100 M. Street, N.W.
Washington, DC, 20037
$1.95

A book designed primarily for local governmental officials, it is also useful for citizen groups. Areas covered include the various uses of surveys; their dangers and how to reduce them, a brief overview and comparison of survey procedures, survey costs and possible funding sources, and illustrations of various types.

Studying Your Community

Roland L. Warren
Published by the Free Press
$4.95

A working manual for laymen and people working in community service. It deals with how to find out about your community in everything from background and setting, housing, education, to health, provisions for special groups, intergroup relations, etc. Included are nearly 2,000 questions to ask when dealing with different aspects of the community, as well as methods and procedures for conducting a community survey.

Where It's At

Jill M. Hamberg, et. al.
Published by New England Free Press
60 Union Square
Somerville, MA, 02143
$1.25 (postage included).

A useful guide to local-level information sources, aimed at helping citizens document their positions. Sections on housing, politics, poverty programs, public services, health, welfare, police/legal system, consumer action, education, business and industry, unions, and jobs. A list of other New England Free Press Publications is also available.

10. Resource Organizations

Center for Community Change
1000 Wisconsin Ave., N.W.
Washington, D.C. 20007
Address requests for publications to: Eileen Paul, Editor
(202) 338-6310

Concerned with national issues affecting the poor and disvantaged, and federal programs designed to deal with these issues. Provides technical assistance in the areas of housing, manpower, and economic development for urban and rural areas.

Publications include: **Citizen Involvement in Community Change: An Opportunity and Challenge** which describes who is eligible for block grants and how to get them. Also has a section on other resource materials. 28pp. $1.50 1976.
Citizen's Action Guide: Monitoring Community Development Block Grants 10pp. $.50
Welfare Reform: Alternative Strategies
General Revenue Sharing: Influencing Local Budgets $1.00

Newsletter: **The Monitor**, bi-monthly, $10/year (local non-profit community groups with limited funds may be exempted from the subscription charge). Good for keeping up with what the federal government is doing with various programs.

Citizen Involvement Training Project
Division of Continuing Education
University of Massachusetts
Amherst, MA 01003
(413) 549-4970

Citizen Involvement Training Project provides workshops, training materials, and consulting, aimed at increasing the effectiveness of citizen groups. CITP's series of citizen training manuals include, in addition to this one,
Power: A Repossesion Manual, by Greg Speeter — a guide to organizing theory and practice, with planning guides and other activities to help a citizen group acquire organizing skills.
Planning, for a Change, by Duane Dale and Nancy Mitiguy — a guide to creative planning and program development for citizen groups, with step-by-step procedures and training excerises.
The Rich Get Richer and the Poor Write Proposals, by Nancy Mitiguy — practical information on effective fund-raising practices, plus a theoretical overview of the difficulties of raising money for worthy causes.
Other manuals in the CITP series will cover group process, state and local government, the use of media for social change, and a trainer's guide for action-oriented citizen education. CITP began in 1976 under a grant from the W.K. Kellogg Foundation.

Community Action Training
128 West State Street
Trenton, N.J. 08608
(609) 393-3746

A private corporation whose purpose is to assist public agencies in training their employees for maximum performance. Types of training range from organizational development to basic office skills. Have a variety of low cost self-study publications.

Publications include: **How to Conduct a Community Action Meeting**. A fold-out chart and clear guide on procedures for conducting a meeting efficiently and with full participation. $.50.
Organizing Groups: A Guide for the Organizer. A book on the various stages a group goes through and the problems it may encounter. Gives suggestions on what the organizer can do. Describes common pitfalls and suggests remedies. $1.50.
Citizen Participation: A Casebook for Democracy. A 365-page book which includes 18 monographs and essays on community problem-solving. $2.95.
Organizing Credit Unions. This handbook outlines a step-by-step process of how to organize a credit union. $1.50.
Tenant Action. A handbook on how to start and carry out a tenant action program. Includes helpful worksheets for the tenant organizer. $1.50.

Institute for Local Self-Reliance
1717 18th Street, N.W.
Washington, D.C. 20009
(202) 232-4108

Established to investigate the technical feasibility of community self-reliance in urban areas. Provides technical assistance to municipalities and community organizations in areas of municipal waste management, municipal finance, urban energy resources, urban food production, and community housing.
Publications: Send for list.
Newsletter: **Self-Reliance**, monthly. Individuals $6.00/year, institutions $12/year, sample copies $.50.
Membership: Individuals $25, Institutions $40 — includes subscription to the newsletter and a 20% discount on publications.

Institute for Responsive Education
775 Commonwealth Avenue
Boston, MA 02215

Publications and assistance especially directed toward citizens working toward better and more responsive schools.

League of Women Voters of the United States
1730 M Street, N.W.
Washington, D.C. 20036
(202) 296–1770

Offers a variety of inexpensive publications around various issues ranging from natural resources and urban crises to public relations and money—making. Facts and Issues publications present a review of the pros and cons of various issues. A variety of community action guides — chiefly how-to-do-it handbooks — are also available.
Publications: Send for list.

National Center for Voluntary Action
1785 Massachusetts Ave., N.W.
Washington, D.C. 20036
(202) 467–5560.

Serves as a principal national source of information on successful programs involving volunteers and assists in the development of volunteer service centers in communities around the nation. Services include consultation and the collection, analysis, and distribution of information on various aspects of volunteering and volunteer management.
Publications; **NCVA Technical Services** lists materials and services offered by NCVA's Technical Services Division. **Help is on the Way** explains how to request services from NCVA's consultant network. Both brochures are free. Publications relevant to the development of citizen groups include **Reference lists: Administration and Organization Communications and Public Relations Community Services Funding, Funding, Fund-raising, and Related Resources**
References lists are available free of charge. Other publications include: **Local Fund Development** 44pp. $1.50
Telling Your Story — Ideas for Local Publicity 22pp. $1.50
Community Needs and Resources Assessment Guidebook 32pp. $.50.
Recruitment of Low–Income Volunteers 23pp. $.50.
NCVA 6-Step Approach to Problem Solving 8pp. $.50
Tips from the "Start-Ups" — suggestions based on the experience of 19 new Volunteer Action Centers, 6-panel foldout, free.
Recruiting Volunteers: Views, Techniques and Comments 24pp. $1.50.

National Citizen Participation Council
1620 Eye Street, N.W., Suite 517
Washington, D.C. 20006
(202) 293-7351

A nonprofit organization dedicated to promoting citizen participation and involvement in the development of federal policy for urban and community program.

Operates 10 regional centers which geographically parallel the Department of Housing and Urban Development regions. Services include: technical assistance and training to regional and local citizen participation groups; including information on specific federally funded programs and assistance in analyzing and interpreting federal regulations and legislations; maintains a library and citizen information and referral service.

National Information Center on Volunteerism
P.O. Box 4179
Boulder, Colorado 80302
(303) 447-0492

An organization concerned with maximizing the effectiveness of, and involving more people in volunteer programs and citizen involvement efforts. Provides technical assistance, information services, consultation, leadership training, and program evaluation.

Publications: Besides information on the development and maintenance and evaluation of volunteer programs, the National Information Center on Volunteerism has some good books on running meetings, and community change work.

Send for their publications brochure.

Newsletter: **Voluntary Action Leadership** (published in conjunction with the National Center for Voluntary Action), quarterly, $8/year.

The National Self-Help Resource Center
2000 S Street, N.W.
Washington, D.C. 20009
(202) 338-5704

The National Self-Help Resource Center is seeking to build linkages between local self-help initiatives willing to aid in the development of a cooperative exchange of information and resources. Serves a national network of community resource centers and related organizations through the National CRC (Community Resource Center) with information resources, publications, technical assistance, consultation and training.

Newsletter: **Exchange**, quarterly; **Network Notes**, monthly, to membership.

Membership: Active CRC's $20; Associate members locally-based neighborhood organizations or special-interest resource centers, $15; individuals $10; governmental agencies professional, civic or human service organizations, $35.

National Training and Information Center
121 W. Superior Street
Chicago, Illinois 60610
(312) 751-1601

Provides technical assistance, training, information, and consultation for community groups who are organizing to determine the future of their communities.

Publications: **Dynamics of Organizing** by Shel Trapp 26 pp. $2.00
How to Use the Home Mortgage Disclosure Act $2.00
Lending Policies Exposed- A Prime Factor in Neighborhood Design $2.00

Support Center
1424 16th Street, N.W.
Washington, D.C. 20036
(202) 256-2443

Seeks to increase the effectiveness of nonprofit public interest organizations. Some of their services include help in the areas of financial and office management, management systems, management planning, personnel (including volunteers), and communications and financial development. Also performs organizational audits and short "check-ups."

The Urban Institute
2100 M Street NW
Washington, D.C. 20037

An independent, nonpartisan, nonprofit research organization. Its free **Publications Catalog** lists the Institute's research reports and and interpretive essays in such areas as policy analysis, program evaluation, transportation, health, land use, housing, urban public finance, criminal justice, and urban economic development. Publications include:

Citizen Involvement in Land Use Governance: Issues and Methods by Nelson M. Rosenbaum, 1976, 100 pp. $3.50.

Presents a framework for the planning and evaluation of citizen involvement programs, focusing on the components of public preparation, citizen participation, and governmental accountability. Illustrates some methods and techniques of involvement that have previously been used and evaluation of their applicability and effectiveness to specific situations.

Measuring Impacts of Land Development: An Initial Approach by Phillip S. Schaenman and Thomas Muller, 1974, 93pp., $2.95.

This report outlines an approach to estimating the impacts of land development on economic, environmental, housing, aesthetic, public and private services, and social concerns. The emphasis is on the evaluation of proposed projects, but portions are applicable to comprehensive planning and evaluating past development.

Para-Transit: A Summary Assessment of Experience and Potential by Ronald F. Kirby, 1974, 34pp., $1.95.

Explores solutions to transportation problems which lie between conventional transit systems and the private automobile, including dial-a-ride services, car pooling, van pools, subscription buses, hire and drive services, etc. Provides a brief summary of the longer report, **Para-Transit: A Neglected Option for Urban Mobility** by Kirby and others, also available from the Urban Institute ($4.95).

Redistribution through Public Choice by Harold M. Hochman and George Peterson, eds.,1974, 368 pp., $12.50.

A collection of essays on income distribution, including analyses of the distribution effects of economic policies, how citizens can express their demand for income redistribution, how elected officials can respond to such demands, and how policies undertaken to enhance economic efficiency may have unintended effects on the distribution of wealth.

Urban Planning Aid, Inc.
Room 305
2 Park Square
Boston, MA 02116
(617) 482-6695

Provides technical assistance and resource materials to low income groups seeking to improve their working and living conditions. Aim is to provide back-up support. Focus is on health and safety, media use, research (social, political, and economic questions) and housing.

11. Other Bibliographies

Citizen Participation in Transportation Planning: A Selected Bibliography by Richard Yukubousky, N.Y. State Dept. of Transportation in cooperation with the U.S. Dept. of Transportation, 1973, 55 pp. Available from U.S. DOT, Federal Highway Administration, Office of Highway Planning, Washington, D.C. 20590, Free.

The literature review section considers the goals and desirability of citizen participation and the characteristics of persons likely to participate in the political process and in voluntary organizations. The bibliography is selectively annotated and has sections on planning participation, political participation, community interaction techniques, citizen participation in transportation planning and other government programs, and a section on other bibliographies.

Exchange Bibliography Series
Council of Planning Librarians
P.O. Box 229
Monticello, IL 61856.

The series covers a wide range of planning and public policy topics. They are available in many libraries. Several pertain to citizen involvement.

Rural Development Literature
(Annotated bibliography 1969-75) Southern Rural Development Center, 1976, 81 pp. Available from the Rural Development Service, USDA, Washington, D.C. 20250. Free.

A starting point in obtaining literature and information for program design and implementation. There are seven subject areas which include fire and emergency services, health care delivery, manpower training/vocational education, and rural housing. Also tells how to obtain the publications from lending libraries and how to get photocopies.

> We here highly resolve . . . that this nation, under God, shall have a new birth of freedom; and that government of the people, by the people, for the people, shall not perish from the earth.
>
> – Abraham Lincoln
> Address at Gettysburg
> November 19, 1863